The
INNER WAY
of TENNIS

SPORT & LIFE

Playing the Game from Inside Out

Randall D. Scott 空船

The Inner Way of Tennis, Sport, and Life –
Playing the Game from Inside Out

© 2025 by Randall D. Scott

First Edition Printed in the United States of America

ISBN: 979-8-9937606-0-5
Paperback

Library of Congress Control Number: 2025923933

Cover and layout design by Simon Thompson
Edited by Jonas Kelsch

For more information, comments, or to place orders,
visit **www.innerwaylife.com**
or email **Randall Scott at SCO@innerwaylife.com.**

This book is intended for educational and inspirational
purposes. The author makes no guarantees regarding outcomes
from the practices or perspectives described herein.

PTP-01

Passenger to Pilot
Publishing

Voices from the Court: Acclaim for The Inner Way

Tim Gallway's *The Inner Game of Tennis* emphasized the mental and emotional significances of the game. Coach Scott now has added a new credence and perspective to these cornerstones of the game."
Tom. Parham – North Carolina Sports Hall of Fame Inductee – Distinguished College Coach

Highly recommended reading for tennis coaches, players and their parents. Over the past two decades tennis has rapidly evolved in areas of stroke technique, fitness training, diet, analytics and racquet and string technology. Randall's book addresses perhaps the last frontier and one of the most important for player development – mental strength and managing stress and one's emotions. Unfortunately, we still regularly see players smashing racquets, yelling at their player's boxes, crying, looks of anguish and taking breaks for mental health. Players regularly say they just want to enjoy tennis and play happily. How to do that? Read Randy's book.
John Reade – Former PBI Professional & Business Development Director

Anyone who has played or coached tennis knows that what separates champions is their ability to access powerful mental and emotional states. Yet most coaching still focuses primarily on technique, overlooking the inner state that produces true flow—the Zone. Randall clearly and practically shows players and coaches how to recognize and enter this state of peace and clarity. Through real-world examples and timeless insights, he demonstrates how inner mastery developed on the court extends far beyond tennis into life itself. By shifting focus from results to continual growth, performance improves naturally— and so does enjoyment. This book offers meaningful guideposts for anyone seeking excellence from the inside out.
Ted Murray – Veteran coach & Author of Tennis from the Heart: Pursuing the Dream

The Inner Way of Tennis is a must-read for coaches and players who are serious about meaningful, mindful excellence "from the Inside Out." It invites total participation in the present moment—free of judgment and attachment to outcomes—and beautifully captures what it means to truly be in the Zone. Thank you, Randy, for putting these timeless insights into words.

Mike "Spike" Collier - PGA Professional

This book is packed with wisdom and mental tools that can transform your game. Coach Randy's method of *"Playing the Game from Inside Out"* has guided me to enjoy tennis more while performing at a higher level. One standout section, *The Four A's*—Acknowledge, Accept, Anchor, Adjust—gives a simple, effective way to reset during a match. Every player, at any level, will benefit from the insights in this book.

Lindley Oler - Accomplished Junior Player -
High School Conference Champion

I've had the privilege of following the development of this book for the past seven years. Like many athletes, the mental side of competition was my greatest limiting factor. Through Randy's clear and practical approach to the inner game, I've seen meaningful improvement in my performance in tennis, pickleball, and racquetball. I've also applied these principles in coaching conference champions, state champions, and high school All-Americans. The insights in this book produce real results. Every athlete, coach, and parent will benefit from this powerful and transformative read.

James Krege - Former Collegiate Player & Accomplished High School Coach

This book perfectly encapsulates a lifetime's worth of wisdom and expertise into an enjoyable, easy-to-read experience. I have two children who play tennis competitively, and as parents, we all want our children to succeed. Yet Western society's focus on outcomes and results can often be counterproductive to true learning and enjoyment, ultimately limiting potential. When we take our children to sporting events, the first question we're almost always asked is, "Did they win, and what was the score?"—and without thinking, we all judge based on wins and losses, winners and errors, makes and misses. This book has increased my awareness of my result-oriented mindset and shown me how this mindset can stifle true growth and understanding, helping me be a better tennis parent.

Morgan Danford – Tennis Parent

I read Tim Gallwey's seminal book, "The Inner Game of Tennis" some years ago, and it still stands the test of time. The author of "The Inner Way of Tennis, Sport and Life" has taken Galway's framework to the next level. Written both anecdotally, and with a nod from history (Alan Watts to name just one...), Randall Scott has managed to bring a fresh perspective to the truly last frontier in the world, our brain and the inner psychology the folks like Joe Dispenza, Tony Robbins, and other giants in that realm have articulated...I highly recommend this read, as the author has crystallized the key points, and highlighted the trouble areas all of those in sport, business and life general face every day...excellent read!

Jim McGarry – Former PBI Professional & Experienced Player-Development Coach

Contents

Acknowledgments

First and foremost, I offer my deepest gratitude to the thousands of players who placed their confidence in me throughout their tennis journeys. Your dedication and openness not only enriched my career but shaped my life in ways words cannot fully express. I am forever indebted to you for inspiring this book and for the opportunity to grow alongside you. A heartfelt thanks also to the many parents who entrusted me with their children, granting me the honor of helping shape not only their tennis skills but their character and inner approach to the game and life.

I extend my sincere thanks to Peter Burwash International (PBI) for the opportunity to be part of one of the truly unique and exceptional organizations—not just in the tennis industry, but in any field. I'm especially grateful to the entire team of PBI professionals, whose influence was pivotal in my growth as a tennis professional and in the creation of this book. In particular, I am deeply thankful for the time I spent with Peter Burwash himself, both at Camp Manitou Wabing and throughout my years with PBI. His insights—on tennis and on life—were nothing short of transformative.

A special acknowledgment goes to my fellow PBI professional and dear friend, Joel Johnson. Joel has been an unwavering source of inspiration since our high school days, nurturing my passion for tennis and guiding me along the path of the "inner way," on and off the court. I will forever be thankful for his invitation to join him at Manitou Wabing in Canada, a pivotal moment in my journey.

I would also like to thank Paul Dale, whose guidance was instrumental in helping me transition into Asia, particularly through my work in

Thailand. His mentorship and the conversations we shared about tennis and coaching directly influenced the content and philosophy of this book, and I am grateful for his ongoing support.

I must also acknowledge the profound influence of Asian spiritual and philosophical traditions—Zen, Buddhism, and Taoism—on my journey. The wisdom found in these traditions, and the countless writings from their teachings, have been a guiding force throughout my life. I am especially indebted to the works of Alan Watts, Thomas Cleary, Eugen Herrigel, Shunryu Suzuki, Kenneth Kushner, Timothy Gallwey, and many others, whose insights have shaped my understanding of the mind-body connection in tennis and life. I am also grateful to the teachers within these traditions, those I have had the privilege of learning from in person and those whose writings have illuminated the path.

Finally, I wish to express my profound gratitude to my family— my mother and father, my brother Brian, and my sister Wendy—whose love, encouragement, and empowering belief have laid the foundation for my personal growth. It is this foundation that enabled my transition from *passenger to pilot*. I am also deeply grateful to my wife, Alisa, for her unwavering support: for being the academy "mom," for accompanying me on countless travels, and for tolerating the extended periods of absence that this journey required. Her patience, love, and partnership have been essential to me every step of the way. I am equally thankful to my son, Peem, for his creative contributions in helping design the book cover, and for his enthusiastic support throughout this project. Their love and encouragement have been a steady light along the path.

Preface

Zen, Buddhism, and the Tao of Tennis

Control your mind-emotion or it will control you.

-Chinese Adage

Mastering the Game from the Inside Out

The philosophies of Zen, Buddhism, and Taoism emphasize a path of liberation through awareness. As philosopher Thomas Cleary wrote in *Zen Essence - The Science of Freedom*, "Zen is the essence of Buddhism, freedom is the essence of Zen." In Eric Fromm and D.T. Suzuki's book Zen Buddhism and Psychoanalysis they state: What is the basic aim of Zen? To put it in Suzuki's words: *"Zen in its essence is the art of seeing into the nature of one's being, and it points the way from bondage to freedom. [...] We can say that Zen liberates all the energies properly and naturally stored in each of us, which are in ordinary circumstances cramped and distorted so that they find no adequate channel for activity. [...] It is the object of Zen, therefore, to save us from going crazy or being crippled."*

This notion of Zen freedom is quite different from the freedoms granted to individuals by political institutions. It originates from within, providing a powerful means of personal growth and self-discovery. In the context of tennis, this inner freedom allows players to break free from external pressures and circumvent mental obstructions. It enables them to perform authentically and instinctively on the court. Ultimately, it leads to self-mastery in the game and in life.

During my years in Asia—especially in Thailand, Japan, and China—I adopted simple mindfulness practices that reshaped how I viewed tennis and life. Breathing and meditation exercises helped me become aware of my emotions and take charge of my development as a player.

As I integrated these Eastern methods into my playing and coaching, I saw them as less mystical and more practical. They trained the "*Inner Way*," the invisible yet very real side of tennis, where matches are settled long before the score is decided.

When I mention Zen or Taoist philosophy, I don't mean to be religious. I'm referring to simple practices that help players stay calm, focused, and free from the mental clutter that so often interferes with performance. Writer Thomas Cleary, who translated many Eastern spiritual classics, explains how Zen helps free the mind from conditioned thinking, and opens the door to greater awareness. Like the Tao (or "Way") in Taoism, this freer mindset is fluid, potent, and elusive. As the Taoist sage Lao Tzu said, "*The Tao's inner power is like this: it lets all things come and go effortlessly, without desire.*"

For tennis players, this means staying calm and centered—whether you're winning, losing, or in a tiebreaker. It's about learning how to respond skillfully, not emotionally. When you develop this kind of easeful awareness, distractions like doubt, frustration, or pressure lose their power over you. You stay connected to the match rather than getting pulled away by your meandering thoughts.

Ultimately, this inside-out approach strengthens players' mental resilience and releases them from the pressure to control every outcome. When they learn to flow with the game instead of fight it, they tap into a far more powerful level of performance. This way of playing also nurtures overall mental well-being. It's a time-tested remedy for the inner unrest that can hold athletes back. In the Inner Way, real transformation begins with awareness: of the mind, body, ball, court, and opponent.

As awareness grows, players take ownership of their game both mentally and physically. They evolve from needing a coach, to becoming their own coach.

For facilitators, drawing on these philosophies can **empower** players to boost their awareness and bring a resilient and adaptive attitude to the game.

Sadly, many players—especially in the West—never fully develop this Inner Way. Western tennis places stresses technique, tactics, and physical training, while the mental side is often an afterthought. This imbalance causes many highly skilled players to struggle under pressure and fail to perform consistently.

Thankfully, that's starting to change. More coaches, parents, and players are beginning to see the importance of mental training. They now recognize that a player's mindset can be just as important—sometimes even more important—than their strokes or fitness. They're realizing that many of the most effective mental training methods were not developed in cutting-edge sports labs, but refined centuries ago in Eastern traditions.

Today, practices like meditation, breathing, and mindfulness exercises are finding their way into more tennis programs. When combined with solid technical and tactical coaching, these methods give players an optimal system for success—not just in tennis, but in life.

The goal of this book is to shine a light on this inner world. My hope is that players, parents, and coaches will discover the power of developing the outer and inner game. This process is not just about becoming a more skillful tennis player—it's about becoming an empowered person.

My Early Struggles: Lessons from Failure

I wasn't born with this mindset. My early years as a player were filled with frustration and emotional blow-ups. Two particularly embarrassing incidents reveal how inept I was at handling the mental and emotional battles that shaped my performance.

The Tree Story

My first memory of poorly playing the unseen game dates back to a high school match against a close friend and practice partner. Unlike me, he did not live and breathe tennis every day. As expected, I dominated the match early on. Midway through, he broke his racket strings. Since I had multiple rackets (and he was my friend), I hesitantly lent him one of mine. Once we resumed, the momentum shifted. He began winning points, then games, and ultimately, the match.

As my lead slipped away, my emotions boiled over. By the time I lost in the third set, I was in a mental tailspin. Barely managing to shake his hand at the net, I turned away in a fit of rage and hurled my returned racket over the fence. Mortified, I watched it spin through the air and land in the top of a tree. Suddenly, my humiliation over losing the match paled in comparison to the embarrassment of having to climb the tree to retrieve my racket.

The Broken Rackets Story

The second incident was equally painful. After a high school dual match, I suffered an unexpected loss to a player I had easily beaten before. Fuming, I stormed off the court, ripped two of my three wooden rackets from my bag. I propped them against a wall, and without a second thought, karate-kicked them in half.

The sight of my shattered rackets—the ones I had worked tirelessly to buy with my paper route money—snapped me out of my sulky state. As I stood there staring at the pieces, I realized the depth of my emotional volatility.

Discovering the Inner Way

At the time I had no coach to help guide me through the emotional flux of adolescence, but in hindsight this disadvantage was a blessing. I was forced to look inward and find the root causes of my struggles. My search eventually led me to the Eastern traditions of Zen Buddhism, Taoism, and ancient mental training techniques.

As I stepped back from my ego and focused on my breath, I understood that when you master your inner game, the outer game will naturally follow. These lessons didn't just help my tennis, they helped me live better. Pursuing The Inner Way of Tennis has inspired me to coach hundreds of others how to master their mental game before it masters them.

I believe this inner path is open to every player, coach, and parent—no matter your current skill level or age. If you approach the concepts in this book with an open mind, I have no doubt you'll experience the liberating power of playing the game from the inside out.

Why I Wrote This Book

This book was written to help tennis players—and anyone facing life's challenges—cultivate better mental wellness, both on and off the court. In a time when stress, pressure, and mental health struggles affect so many, these pages offer tools to strengthen your inner game.

Through the practices in this book, you'll learn how to:

- Stay calm under pressure
- Reset quickly after mistakes
- Handle emotions with awareness and clarity
- Play with an empowering, resilient attitude
- Build deep self-trust from the inside out
- Beyond performance, this book supports your overall mental wellness, offering a pathway to more ease, freedom, and joy
  — on the court and in life.

In tennis today—as in sport and life—many players openly speak about their struggles with mental health. This book is written to meet that need. The principles within are designed to support genuine mental wellness, offering ease in place of the inner turmoil and mental dis-ease so many experience. Through understanding and practice, the reader is guided toward a calmer, more grounded way of playing and living.

Introduction
The Inner Way of Tennis in the Kingdoms

How far the pupil will go is not the concern of the teacher and Master. Hardly has he shown him the right way when he must let him go on alone."

- Eugen Herrigel, Zen in the Art of Archery

My journey to becoming a facilitator and discovering the Inner Way began nearly four decades ago, when my two passions, tennis and philosophy, first came together. As a freshman philosophy student at the University of North Carolina - Chapel Hill, and with my tennis game still struggling, I found myself at a crossroads. It was then I began to see how my philosophical pursuits could complement and transform my development as a tennis player. Making this connection sparked within me a desire to illuminate the hidden game—not just the match between player and opponent, but the game that takes place within the mind and spirit.

The *Inner Way of Tennis* is a path that leads players to what's often called 'the Zone.' Coaches, sports psychologists, and parents all mention the Zone when trying to help players with their mindset. But even those who have entered this state of flow often struggle to describe it—let alone guide others how to enter it at will.

My pursuit of the Zone, and the inner path that leads to it, deepened in college—especially during five unforgettable summers coaching at Camp Manitou-Wabing in the Canadian wilderness.

Awakening at Manitou

Camp Manitou was more than just a summer job. Nestled in Canada's breathtaking lake country, it was a spiritual place. Since long before the camp existed, local indigenous tribes have regarded the land as sacred. They believe the natural world is unified by a life force they call *maenitu* or *monetoo*—"Great Spirit."

At Manitou I was immersed in the deep Northwoods. Chipmunks would wander into our office, and we would feed them sunflower seeds by hand. On some nights I had the pleasure of seeing the aurora light up the Canadian summer sky. In these moments I could feel a deep connection to nature and the oneness of the experience. Later I would see how this kinship with the natural world intertwines with the philosophies I would explore across Asia—in Thailand, Japan, China, and India.

The opportunity to coach at Camp Manitou opened after my freshman year at Elon College. My longtime practice partner and close friend, Joel Johnson, who had worked there the previous summer, invited me to join the camp tennis staff. I spent five summers at Manitou—years that helped me grow as a coach and as a player and taught me how to steer my own journey.

Becoming the Pilot

Those formative summers showed me that too often I had been a passenger on my own journey. I passively rode out life's rough patches when I could have taken the helm.

My transition from passenger to pilot began with an intensive two-week session to prepare coaches at Camp Manitou. The training philosophy was simple but profound: guide players to become their own coach.

The program had been created by Peter Burwash, a passionate and forward-thinking coach who believed that self-sufficiency should be the ultimate goal for every athlete. He often said: "Whether you want to or not, you must eventually learn to coach yourself... Your goal should be to become a self-sufficient tennis player so you can win even when your strokes desert you."

That summer I started to feel what he meant. In one match, I kept hitting my forehand into the net. But rather than go into emotional autopilot, I recalled a simple instruction Peter had delivered in training: "hit higher over the net." I made the adjustment and started landing more shots.

By staying cool and aware, I was improving my game through self-coaching. In fact, I'd been self-coaching throughout my tennis career—just not always consciously.

The Lesson That Changed Everything

During a training session with over fifty coaches, Joel volunteered me for a one-on-one lesson with Peter Burwash. We worked on my forehand, and in less than ten minutes, my stroke improved significantly.

In that short lesson, the most important change was not in my stroke, but my awareness of racket and body. By guiding me to pay attention and take control, Peter had handed me the keys to my own progression.

From then on, I committed to this independent-minded approach—not just to improve myself, but to help hundreds of other players find their own path to self-mastery.

The Road to Self-Coaching

Even after my landmark lesson with Peter, I still often felt like a passenger on my tennis journey. It wasn't until I tried out for the Elon College men's tennis team when I had a breakthrough.

I knew the odds of making the Elon team were slim, but I was willing to take the risk. When I arrived at tryouts, I was surprised to see Coach Tom Parham in charge. He had already filled most of the roster, including his scholarship players. Five players were vying for the last spot.

Coach Parham was a man I had trained with years prior—first at his summer camp, and later in private lessons. After one of our lessons, he told me I probably wasn't college-level material. On the way home I sat in the back seat of the car, sobbing the whole way. It felt like my dream was over. I stopped taking lessons from Coach Parham—not out of anger, but to protect what little belief I had left in myself. I decided the way forward was to double down on my self-coaching.

At the Elon tryouts, I focused on what I could control: my attitude, effort, and energy. I pushed myself in every drill, every match, every sprint. By the last day of tryouts, several players had dropped out. When the final roster was posted, I found my name at the very bottom of the list. Although I had several colleges to choose from, including UNC - Chapel Hill, joining the Elon team meant everything to me. Not just because I'd made the team, but because I had refused to let go of my belief. I had stepped into the pilot's seat.

Years later, as a coach, I understood that Coach Parham had not meant to discourage me after that lesson. The experience showed me that facilitators must walk a line between truth and belief when instructing impressionable young players.

From the Outer Game to the Inner Way

After transferring to UNC-Chapel Hill and finishing my final summer at Manitou, I began my professional career with Peter Burwash International. My first assignment was at the Guam Hilton, directing their tennis program. Over the next five years, I worked on refining everything I'd learned about the Inner Way. Later, I co-founded a tennis academy in Bangkok, coaching top-level juniors in national and international events. It was during this time that I started to appreciate something vital: When competing, players spend more time *not* hitting the ball.

According to a Wall Street Journal study, the ball is in play only 17.5% of a match. The vast majority of the match happens in the space between points, when players are pacing, sitting, and thinking. If a player is not trained to manage this hidden game, they are vulnerable to stress, overthinking, and collapse under pressure.

This is where the Inner Way comes in. It's not just about making contact with the ball. It's about staying mentally present and aligned in the in-between space, where the real contest often takes place.

Seeing Through the Ego

As my playing and facilitating progressed, so did my studies. I began to question some of the essential ideas behind Western sports psychology. While techniques like positive self-talk, Cognitive Behavioral Therapy (CBT), and Neuro-Linguistic Programming (NLP) can help stabilize the mind in the short term, they often fall apart when a player is flooded by intense emotional patterns like self-doubt, fear, or frustration. These methods generally approach the ego as something to manage, correct, or control.

But in my experience, the ego itself is the problem—the very source of the inner turbulence. Real freedom comes not from strengthening or negotiating with the ego, but from seeing through it and loosening its grip entirely.

Drawing from Taoism, Zen, and other Eastern philosophical traditions, I came to see that trying to "fix" the ego often reinforces its control. What's needed is not management, it's freedom from the illusion of the ego-self.

Coach Timothy Gallwey's concept of the two selves—one that micromanages our behavior, and the other that reacts intuitively— has become a popular mental training concept in tennis and the wider sports world.. While Gallwey's notion of Self 1 and Self 2 was a good start, both identities are still caught up with the ego. Real transformation does not come from distracting the mind; it comes from seeing that the ego itself is not really you.

Moving Past the Ego

Taoist thinker Wei Wu Wei seemed to understand this in his book *All Else Is Bondage*: "*Has one not realized that a 'self' is only one's object, perceptual and conceptual, and that it could not be what we are?*"

Many struggling players bring a confused identity to the court. They think they must perform in order to be worthy. But this ego-centric belief is what blocks them from entering the Zone.

Gallwey understood this, but his solution was incomplete. The answer is not Self 1 vs. Self 2—it's more like **Self vs. No-Self**. True flow happens when players are free from judgment, fear, and expectation. When they are **present**, alive, and open, they can play in the Zone.

The Path Ahead

The Inner Way of Tennis goes beyond controlling your thoughts and toughing it out. It's about **seeing through the ego**, letting go of the noise, and playing with freedom. It's about knowing when to stop trying and start **trusting**. It's about becoming pilot of your own progress.

This book will guide you through that journey—whether you're a player, parent, or coach—so you can build the whole game: not just the one others see, but the one only you can see.

It's time to step into the pilot's seat. Let's begin.

Part One

The Inner Way:
Foundations

In the opening sections, I explored the essence of the Inner Way, a holistic approach to tennis that goes beyond physical technique and strategic thinking. It is a path that aligns **mind, body, and spirit**, helping players approach the game from the inside out.

In this section we can explore the fundamentals of this approach: **attitude** and **awareness**.

At the core of the Inner Way is the ability to **cultivate an empowering attitude** and practice **nonjudgmental awareness**. These two fundamentals shape a player's inner game, giving them the mental balance and resilience to thrive in competition.

Timothy Gallwey, pioneer of the Inner Game philosophy, wrote: *"Judgment results in tightness, and tightness interferes with the fluidity required for accurate and quick movement. Relaxation produces smooth strokes and results from accepting your strokes as they are, even if erratic."*

He proposed that players have two selves: a critical, controlling Self 1 and a spontaneous, capable Self 2. To let Self 2 "take charge," he explained, Self 1 must be gently distracted so it no longer interferes with natural ability.

The Inner Way has a different focus. Rather than centering the conversation around Self 1 and Self 2, it turns attention to the more fundamental issue: the habit of identifying with a "self" at all. When players stop identifying with the ego-self and instead experience a state of no-self, they naturally enter a mind-frame of calmness, playfulness, and adaptability. This inner game must be practiced as deliberately as the outer one—developed alongside footwork, mechanics, and strategy. Without a trained inner structure, even highly skilled athletes can unravel under pressure. I've seen this at every level, from beginners to professionals.Although coaches, parents, and players often say attitude matters, few understand how it truly shapes performance, and even fewer know how to cultivate an empowering one. Well-meaning guidance can unintentionally reinforce limiting attitudes.The Inner Way offers a clear, structured approach to building a mindset that supports genuine growth and peak performance.

Programing the Mind: Early Foundations

Developing the foundations of attitude and awareness is essential—not just for tennis, but for a player's growth as a human being. Those responsible for shaping a young athlete's mind must do so with care, clarity, and consistency. Throughout my career, I have witnessed the difficulty of reversing entrenched negative beliefs. The key is to understand that mental obstacles are best addressed through proactive conditioning than reactive correction.

Psychologists generally agree that a child's core beliefs, attitudes, and personality traits largely form between the ages of 2 and 8. During these years, their mental worlds are shaped by their families, communities, media, teachers, and peers. Even before they can talk, they begin absorbing messages about themselves and the world.

Their early experiences lay the groundwork for their beliefs about effort, failure, competition, and success. This shaping is especially evident in an individual sport like tennis, where early exposure to certain narratives can dictate a player's beliefs, capabilities, and performance.

My travels, philosophical and spiritual studies, and life experiences have revealed the constraints of my mental conditioning and given me insight into how these factors adversely affected my tennis game.

As I've observed in my work with players in Asia, cultural narratives greatly influence attitude. For example, Japanese players tend to show a strong work ethic and persistence, as these qualities are highly valued in Japanese culture. Indian players demonstrate exceptional commitment and discipline; Chinese players resilience and a calm intensity; and Thai players approach the game with a sense of equanimity and playfulness.

These attributes are empowering and shaped by cultural conditioning. If a player grows up surrounded by criticism, fear, or pressure, negative attitudes easily take root. The older they get, the harder it becomes to uproot these attitudes.

The Perception-Projection Loop in Tennis
"You can twist perceptions, Reality won't budge."

– Neil Peart

I believe it is essential for players, coaches, and parents to understand how our conditioned beliefs and behaviors shape our on-court performance, and vice versa. This process forms a cycle I call the perception-projection loop. It often leads players to unconscious behaviors that can significantly impact their performance in matches. As discussed above, players absorb narratives about success, failure, and their own abilities from a young age. If a player who loses a match perceives themselves as 'not good enough,' that thought can project onto their next performance in the form of hesitance or fear of failure. As they step onto the court, their mind might replay past mistakes. This can cause them to be tight in their strokes, second-guess their shots, and ultimately perform poorly. Essentially, they sabotage their game before it even begins.

Whereas an empowering perception can create a more encouraging feedback loop. If a player views setbacks as opportunities for growth—like reflecting on how they learned from a challenging match—they are likely to enter their next game with confidence and resilience. An optimistic mindset allows them to project strong energy, leading to focused performance. So if they do miss a critical serve, they might visualize the next serve as successful, and follow through. A perception shift can enhance their overall game, leading not only to better performance but also a more enjoyable playing experience.

The cycle of perception and projection begins early in one's tennis journey. Wanting to impress parents or coaches can create pressure that leads to disempowering beliefs, such as 'I can't disappoint them' or 'I have to win to be good enough.' Such thoughts can loop through a player's mind, creating anxiety that inhibits their focus on court. When the pressure mounts, they might struggle to concentrate, their shots become erratic, and their performance suffers dramatically.

Breaking out of this disempowering loop requires awareness. The first step towards awareness is recognizing that these patterns exist. For a tennis player, acknowledging that their mindset may be impeding their performance is crucial. Once they see the loop for what it is, they can start to break its influence.

Staying present and focused is key to disrupting the perception-projection loop. Instead of worrying about past matches or future outcomes, players can use simple tools such as concentrating on their breathing, feeling their grip, and listening to the contact. Maintaining this awareness makes negative thoughts irrelevant and easier to release. Rather than succumbing to anxiety over a potential fault, players can soothe their nerves with a simple mantra like "Toss-hit," "Bounce-contact," or my personal favorite: "Every day, in every way, my serve, forehand, volley, movement, and skills are getting better and better." As players cultivate awareness, they become better at choosing empowering perceptions. Instead of viewing their opponent as a challenger, they see them as a partner in challenge who promotes their growth. The perception shift allows them to control the narrative and edit out self-limiting beliefs like competition anxiety.

However, breaking free from negative thought patterns may require a difficult period of introspection and self-questioning. A tennis player might need to confront the pressures they feel from external sources—including coaches, parents, and peers—as well as the expectations they place on themselves. Self-reflection can also reveal underlying fears, like the fear of failure or the fear of disappointing others.

As players confront oppressive thoughts, they can clarify their motivations and goals. They can distinguish between what truly drives them in the sport, and what is imposed on them. They can then work on replacing debilitating beliefs with a more constructive outlook. Ultimately, this reprograming helps them connect more deeply to their passion for tennis. It allows them to play more authentically and with greater joy, regardless of the pressures surrounding them.

With awareness as their guiding principle, players can step onto the court not merely as competitors, but as pilots of their mental and emotional journey. They are ready to navigate the complexities of performance with confidence and clarity.

But the roots of disempowering beliefs run even deeper than cultural programing. Many players unknowingly base their sense of self on what they do on court. This can create a fragile 'ego system' that crumbles under pressure.

The Lie of "I"

In tennis as in life, players often struggle with something deeper than forehands and footwork. *It's the tension between loving who they think they are and disliking that same image.* On the tennis court, the "lie" shows up when players think their value depends on how well they look or perform. Their self-worth gets tied up with things like results, rankings, and reputation. Some players build their whole identity around what they've accomplished, while others doubt themselves constantly. Many do both.

Think of yourself like an actor in a movie. An actor fully commits to playing a character. They speak like them, move like them, feel like them. While the camera is rolling, they are that character. But here's the key: they never forget they aren't actually the character. When the camera turns off, they stop pretending. They don't carry the role home. They don't protect the character's image. They don't fear for the character's reputation. They know it was just a role.

Your ego—the "I," the name, the identity, the tennis player—is similar. It's a role you play. The trouble begins when you forget it's a role and believe it is who you are.

German psychologist and philosopher Erich Fromm wrote in *The Sane Society* that "The psychic task which a person can and must set for himself, is not to feel secure, but to be able to tolerate insecurity, without panic and undue fear." This speaks directly to players who tie their self-worth to results, appearance, or reputation. When everything depends on external validation, there is a constant need for security, for certainty.

When you identify completely with the role of "tennis player," every mistake feels personal. You're afraid to miss because you might look bad. You need to win to feel okay. You protect your image. But Fromm suggests that true psychological growth involves embracing insecurity. A tennis player learns to accept not always knowing the outcome, not always winning, and not always being judged favorably—yet still doing their best.

When you play the role without believing you are the role, something softens. You still compete. You still care. But underneath it, you know: this is a character I'm playing right now. That acceptance helps free you from the fear that undermines performance.

The Ego and Identity

For many athletes, identity becomes all about two things: their physical ability and their results—how often they win, what others think, and what titles they have earned. This kind of thinking builds a shaky inner foundation. A player who links their self-image to winning may walk onto the court already anxious—not because of their opponent's skill, but because of the mental weight they're carrying.

It's the weight of protecting the character.

Fromm says that well-being is possible through being rather than having. For tennis players, this points to the power of letting go of ego-identification—releasing the need to protect or prove themselves—and instead immersing fully in the experience of playing.

This does not mean you stop playing the role. The actor still performs with total commitment. But the actor knows they are not the role. In the same way, you can step onto the court fully as "the competitor," while knowing, quietly, that this identity is something you are expressing—not something you are.

When players temporarily drop this identification and simply participate in competition, performance becomes fluid, natural, and even joyful. There is nothing to defend. Nothing to prove. No image to protect. Mistakes are no longer threats to the self—they are simply part of the scene unfolding.

This easeful, enhanced state of performance is captured in Eugen Herrigel's Buddhist classic *Zen in the Art of Archery*: "The archer ceases to be conscious of himself... he becomes one with the perfecting of his technical skill."

Or in plain terms: when you start thinking too much about yourself, you leave the moment.

Being in the natural flow of playing in the here and now involves the temporary dissolution of identification with the self. The body relaxes. The mind quiets. The game begins to play itself. And performance often improves not because you tried harder—but because you stopped carrying yourself so heavily.

A Story of Letting Go: Benjamas

Benjamas (middle) receiving academy sponsorship Randall and Paul Dale to (right)

One player I had the privilege of helping develop was Benjamas, a Thai national competitor who played in the Olympics and reached a career-high ranking of 134 on the WTA Tour.

When she first arrived at our academy, she struggled with a common problem: choking under pressure. As we began to explore her mindset and inner narratives, we discovered that during crucial match moments she would get lost in ego-driven fantasies like: 'If I win, it will be amazing, but if I lose, it will be humiliating.'

This impending praise or embarrassment was taking her mind out of the Zone. It not only hindered her concentration, but it reduced her chances of winning matches and enjoying the game.

By working on her inner game, Benjamas began to recognize these thoughts as ego stories, and not the truth. She started playing less to impress others, and more to express herself. Her performance improved, her joy returned, and she reached the highest levels of the sport. Benjamas' story is a lesson in how freeing oneself from pessimistic narratives and ego constraints can unlock potential.

Sabotage by Ego

Consider another scenario where a talented player is serving for the match. As they prepare, they are consumed by thoughts of how a double fault could damage their reputation. They are distracted from their technique and the match dynamics. They hesitate, second-guess their serve, and, of course they double fault. The ego self—rooted in fear of failure—has hindered them from capitalizing on their training and instinctual skill. Their performance is sabotaged by the pressure to perform.

Most players grow up in systems that reward achievement over authenticity. Media, coaches—even well-meaning parents—often reinforce the idea that *winning equals worth*. As a result, many players carry a false sense of identity—a mask made up of rankings, roles, or praise they have received. They are no longer living in their body but solely in their head—and likely overthinking.

When players attach their identity to results, they become fragile under pressure. Their mental focus shifts from *what they're doing* to *what it all means*. That shift costs them the point, the set—or the whole match. This is not about poor technique. It's about ego fear. They are afraid of losing the image they have built.

But true power comes when you temporarily drop identification with the ego mask, simply being who you are—pure awareness—rather than succumbing to the illusion of "I." When you stop chasing validation and start playing from a place of non-judgmental awareness, without desire for a particular outcome, you perform better and enjoy the game more.

A player grounded in egolessness remains concentrated during critical points—even if they lose. They understand that the point exists only in the here and now and maintain their commitment to play, regardless of what others perceive or project as success or failure. As Michael Jordan famously said, "I've missed more than 9,000 shots in my career. I've lost almost 300 games. Twenty-six times I've been trusted to take the game-winning shot and missed. I've failed over and over and over again in my life. And that is why I succeed."

Failure did not define Jordan, and the fear of failure did not control him. His empowering attitude underscores the importance of non-judgmental awareness in the here and now. By accepting the ups and downs, uncertainties, and chaos of competition, players can develop unshakable confidence.

This rings especially true for tennis players, who must cope with the uncertainties of competition without letting their constructed identities dictate their experience. To enter this "No-Self" state, where they are in tune with the moment, players can use techniques grounded in neuroscience and mindfulness.

Imagine a player who embraces a No-Self perspective. Rather than worrying about how their performance reflects on their identity, they fully immerse themselves in the experience of playing. In other words, uncertainty and insecurity cannot bring them down, because they are not caught in the illusion of "I." Scholar Erich Fromm once wrote "The task we must set for ourselves is not to feel secure, but to be able to tolerate insecurity." In tennis, and all sports, identifying with the ego is the primary source of insecurity. The pressure to perform can amplify this, leading to anxiety and self-doubt. The player quite literally "goes to pieces" under the strain. As Fromm stated in his book *Zen Buddhism and Psychoanalysis*: "Well-being means, finally, to drop one's Ego, to give up greed, to cease chasing after the preservation and the aggrandizement of the Ego, to be and to experience one's self in the act of being, not in having, preserving, coveting, using."

Letting go of ego-identification allows the athlete to exist fully in the act of playing—unstuck from outcomes and driven by presence rather than performance.

Knowing that the ego can be a hindrance helps players foster a mindset for optimal performance. Simple techniques like breathing exercises serve as powerful tools for helping players regain control over their mental state. Below are methods I've employed to help players to shift away from their ego and develop their inner game.

Techniques for Letting Go

- **Breathe deeply:** Diaphragmatic or "belly" breathing calms your system and quiets your mind.
- **Focus on a target:** Lock your eyes onto the ball or a visual cue to stay anchored.
- **Shift your attention:** Notice the sound of the ball, your footsteps, or your breath rhythm.
- **Play one point at a time:** Let go of score and stories. Just play what's in front of you.

By integrating these techniques, players can effectively navigate the uncertainties of tennis while promoting a more constructive relationship with their ego.

When they are in control, players can adopt empowering narratives that enhance their confidence and resilience. They can stay grounded in a clear game plan, and avoid getting lost in doubts or fears.

They can cultivate an empowering attitude and use awareness to release their minds from the ego's grasp. This approach allows them to respond more effectively to the dynamic nature of matches, ultimately enhancing their performance and enjoyment of the sport.

Performing and Being

To truly thrive in tennis, players must question false narratives about identity and success. The more they let go of the "I," the more they gain access to joy, creativity, and peak performance.

Athletes who emphasize *task orientation*—on process, effort, and skill mastery—tend to exhibit intrinsic motivation, resilience, and better overall well-being. In contrast, a strong *ego orientation*—focused on outperforming others—can bring anxiety, boredom, and reliance on luck.

For elite performers, balance is key: combining task and ego orientation can "insulate" each other's downsides and support peak performance. Encouraging athletes to detach from outcome fixation and instead immerse in performance itself aligns with "not identifying with the ego."

A 2022 study explored how mindfulness and nonattachment-to-self (NTS) impact athlete well-being. While they found that both traits may contribute positively to well-being and self-actualization, NTS appeared to play a greater role.

This suggests that athletes who cultivate the ability to "let go" of egoic attachments like outcome obsession can sharpen their focus, experience richer well-being, and perform more authentically.

This is the essence of the Inner Way: not becoming someone better—but remembering who you are when you stop trying to be someone at all.

Steps to Empowerment

Before developing an empowering attitude, it is vital to recognize misguided beliefs that hinder progress. I will share the most common disempowering beliefs I've observed in players throughout my career, and contrast these with the empowering attributes that have unlocked true potential.

The Price of Disempowerment

1. **Avoiding Effort or Failing to Push Oneself in Training**

   Tennis Example: A player who avoids tough drills—like those focused on footwork or high-pressure second serves—arrives at matches unprepared, especially against opponents who exploit those weaknesses. *Benefit of Removing It:* Embracing challenging training builds mental stamina and prepares players to meet adversity head-on during competition.

2. **Reacting with Frustration or Anger After Losing a Point**

   Tennis Example: A player who slams their racquet after losing a game point loses focus and appears emotionally unstable. Contrast this with Novak Djokovic, who resets by breathing and recalibrating his mindset. *Benefit of Removing It:* Learning to recover quickly from mistakes protects performance and keeps players emotionally steady.

3. **Blaming External Factors (weather, surface, referee, etc.)**

   Tennis Example: A player who blames the court for poor footing or the sun for missed overheads starts mentally checking out. In contrast, top players adjust and compete, regardless of the conditions. *Benefit of Removing It:* Accepting uncontrollables fosters adaptability and sharpens a player's ability to adjust under any circumstances.

4. **Overly Self-Critical or Perfectionist Mindset**

   Tennis Example: A perfectionist may freeze under pressure, terrified to make mistakes. Most top players battle this early in their career but grew by shifting their focus toward steady improvement. *Benefit of Removing It:* Releasing perfectionism allows for consistent, confident play and makes room for self-compassion and growth.

5. **Fear of Failure or Avoidance of Risk** *Tennis Example:* Fear of losing leads to tentative play. Rafael Nadal, however, embraces big moments by taking more risk—not less—hitting with heavier spin and going for his shots. *Benefit of Removing It:* Letting go of fear unleashes a player's natural game, encouraging assertiveness and full engagement.

Attributes That Empower

1. Accepting Mistakes as Part of the Learning Process

Tennis Example: Double faults and missed volleys are inevitable. Instead of reacting with frustration, an empowered player analyzes what went wrong and adjusts. *Benefit of Programing It:* Mistakes become lessons. This mindset supports emotional balance and rapid learning.

2. Maintaining Self-Discipline and Consistent Effort

Tennis Example: Players like Rafael Nadal don't just practice during assigned sessions—they stay late, refine details, and train with purpose. *Benefit of Programing It:* Self-discipline builds physical skill and mental toughness, especially when matches get long or challenging.

3. Believing in the Power of Persistence

Tennis Example: A persistent player down 0–5 in a set refuses to quit. Like Novak Djokovic, they fight for every point, knowing the tide can turn at any moment. *Benefit of Programing It:* Persistence creates resilience. The belief that "I can come back" keeps players alive in matches others might quit.

4. Focusing on the Process, Not Just the Outcome

Tennis Example: A player working on their backhand chooses to focus on timing and contact point rather than obsessing about winning. Top players frequently take this approach during recovery phases. *Benefit of Programing It:* Process focus lowers anxiety, strengthens confidence, and allows better execution under pressure.

5. Viewing the Opponent as a Source of Growth

Tennis Example: Instead of resenting tough opponents, an empowered player sees them as fuel for development—like Djokovic, who sees each new challenger as a chance to improve. *Benefit of Programing It:* This perspective replaces comparison with curiosity and competition with cooperation in personal growth.

Every time a player shows up to practice, they're not just working on strokes—they're shaping attitude habits. What they repeat becomes ingrained. The mental fuel they carry into matches will either ignite or clog their performance engine.

Disempowering beliefs limit energy, joy, and freedom.

Empowering attitudes liberate potential and unlock flow.

Helping players move from fear to freedom, from criticism to curiosity, and from control to confidence is one of the greatest gifts a coach, parent, or player can give.

Attitude: The Fuel of Empowerment

The first step on the journey from passenger to empowered player is to understand that our beliefs are not chosen, but absorbed.

Ruth Benedict, a pioneering anthropologist, wrote in her book *Patterns of Culture:* "From the moment of his birth, the customs into which he is born shape his experience and behavior."

Among these customs, language is one of the most important. As children, we absorb the words of those around us, often without question. Over time, the language we receive helps shape our internal belief system.

I didn't realize how deep this programing went until I began studying other cultures and traveling the world. I saw how my upbringing and inherited beliefs had shaped my mindset and my tennis game. Much of this subtext was holding me back on the court.

A classic example of how experience shapes perception is the famous kitten experiment by Blakemore and Cooper in the 1970. Kittens were raised in containers that had only horizontal or vertical lines. Later, they could barely see anything outside those patterns.

Their reality had been shaped—literally—by what they were exposed to. Our mental world is shaped by what we've been raised to see — and *not* to see. If we remain stuck in a narrow realty, we tend to follow old patterns.

These patterns are not just personal—they're cultural. They reflect the values passed down through family, school, and community. And just as positive traits can be nurtured by culture, so can negative ones: fear of failure, self-doubt, perfectionism, or obsession with results.

Some players are born into supportive, resource-rich environments, while others are not. But what I've seen, over and over, is where you start does not define where you will finish. My goal as a facilitator has always been to help players remove disempowering beliefs and cultivate strengths they already possess. I have worked with players who came from very little but rose above their peers through focus, resilience, and belief.

Reclaiming the Inner Way

Unlike the kittens in that old study, we're not slaves to our conditioning. With reflection, guidance, and effort, we can rewrite our inner script. We can transform limiting beliefs into empowering ones. We can move from being passengers, shaped by others' expectations, to pilots who steer our own development.

This shift is what the Inner Way is all about. And it starts with attitude.

Empowerment: Fueling the Inner Engine

Having established that attitude is the mental framework shaping a player's behavior and performance—molded by past experiences and reinforced by the ego—we now turn to the elements that strengthen and support it.

Just as a finely tuned machine requires clean, high-quality fuel to operate at its best, a player's mindset must be built on the right inner ingredients to perform under pressure. These ingredients form what I call the three fundamental characteristics of an empowering attitude—the essential "fuel" for the inner engine of peak performance.

Before exploring these three fundamentals, however, it is crucial to first recognize the most common disempowering beliefs that limit growth and cause players to struggle—beliefs I have witnessed repeatedly throughout my decades of coaching. I will then contrast these with the empowering attributes that replace them, unlocking a player's true potential.

Coach's Corner:

Flow emerges when ego quiets. Watch for signs of ego-driven tension—overthinking, long routines, tight body language—and guide players back to the present. After matches, empower them to reflect with questions like, "What did I learn?" and "Where did I grow?" Awareness drives real transformation.

Player's Note:

Flow happens when you're no longer trying to prove anything. Be present. Breathe. Let the game play through you.

Parent Insight:

Your child is not their ranking. What you celebrate becomes their inner voice—so praise effort, attitude, resilience, and learning, not just results. Help them love the game, not fear it.

Acquiring an Empowering Attitude

I. From Mind-Fullness to Emptiness

*"Just as a river flows, and a mountain stands,
so you are both empty and full. You have access to both
possibilities; you can wander, react, and be carried along by the
current of your own life. To be empty is to be receptive, to be full is
to express your true nature."*

— Alan Watts

The Essence of Emptiness: Freedom from Needless Suffering

At the heart of an empowering attitude lies the principle of emptiness. This practice invites players to let go of ego-based stories—especially the ones centered on "I": "I must win." "I can't lose." "I need to prove myself."

These inner stories are often shaped by past experiences, judgments, and cultural expectations. They create a mental cage that defines how players see themselves—both on and off the court.

By learning to empty the mind of these stories, players can free themselves from the pressure to prove, achieve, or perform for others. In that space of mental clarity, real growth can begin.

Andre Agassi: A Journey into Emptiness

A powerful example of this transformation is the story of Andre Agassi. Early in his career, Agassi faced enormous pressure as a prodigy with a public image to uphold. Fame, expectation, and ego weighed heavily on him.

But as he matured, Agassi began to shed those pressures. In his autobiography, he reflects: "When you chase perfection, when you make perfection the ultimate goal, do you know what you're doing? You're chasing something that doesn't exist. You're making everyone around you miserable. You're making yourself miserable." By releasing who he thought he had to be, Agassi found who he truly was—a tennis player. And that shift allowed him to make a stunning comeback and become one of the most respected and beloved figures in the game.

This is the essence of emptiness: letting go to move forward. In doing so, players open themselves to a more focused and fearless game.

Creating Space for Growth

When a player enters a state of mental emptiness, they're no longer weighed down by self-imposed limits. Judgment fades. Pressure loosens. There's room to breathe. The newfound space becomes a blank canvas— open, fresh, and receptive to growth.

Just as meditation clears the mind and brings one into the present, tennis players can learn to cultivate a similar presence on the court. Every point becomes a moment to reset, not relive past mistakes or entertain fears. It becomes less about competition and more about self-improvement. As Timothy Gallwey writes in *The Inner Game of Tennis*, this game "is played against such obstacles as lapses in concentration, nervousness, self-doubt, and self-condemnation." Essentially, it means playing against yourself.

To play against yourself means to observe your internal narratives, learn from them, and eventually *empty* them. To do that fully means recognizing the deeper truth: that there is no fixed self to defend or protect. This is the key insight that unlocks mental freedom and empowers performance.

The Power of Letting Go

Practicing emptiness also invites players to approach their craft with vulnerability. This means being open to failure, unsure outcomes, and not always having the answers. It means trusting the process—even when the results don't come immediately.

This is what psychologist Carol Dweck describes as a "growth mindset"—where setbacks are opportunities to learn rather than threats to identity. When players internalize this mindset, fear dissolves. Confidence emerges. The court becomes a place of exploration, not just evaluation.

An example of this can be found in the story of Andy Murray. After major injuries and setbacks, Murray faced deep uncertainty about whether he could return to elite form. But instead of clinging to his old identity, he chose to let go. "I was far from perfect," he said in 2024, "but I did a really good job during my career, regardless of the highs and lows. Whether it's winning tournaments or having tough losses or an having an operation, I always came into work with the same dedication and passion as the day before. Regardless of the highs and lows the sport has thrown at me. I always came into work and put in a good day. I gave my best effort. That's what I'm proud of."

By shedding past narratives and expectations, Murray rediscovered his love for the game. His renewed sense of purpose came not from control—but from release.

The Foundation of Empowerment

By releasing ego-based desires, rigid identities, and mental clutter, players begin to unhook from suffering and unlock their natural ability to focus, learn, and enjoy the game. Emptiness, then, is not weakness—it's opportunity. It's the space where learning happens. It gives the mind freedom to reset, recover, and return better.

Emptiness is the first cornerstone of an empowering attitude. It teaches players to let go of stories that create stress, pressure, and doubt. With this clarity, growth becomes fluid. Performance becomes expressive. Tennis becomes fun again. And that's when mastery begins.

From Caterpillar to Butterfly

As athletes, we often get trapped in disempowering beliefs and stories about who we are and what we can or can't do. These beliefs are usually shaped by past experiences, judgments, and outside influences—and they limit our view of what's possible.

Think of a caterpillar. In its early stage, it's limited to crawling and can't imagine flying. It does not yet know it can transform. Many tennis players are the same way. They see themselves only as they are now—defined by past results, rankings, or others' opinions—never realizing their potential to become something much greater.

Coach's Corner:

Don't just coach technique—coach spaciousness. Encourage players to breathe between points, release self-judgment, and reset fully. Awareness is the first skill of mastery.

Player's Note:

When your mind is crowded with "I" thoughts—how you look, what others think, whether you're winning—you shrink. Let them go and you expand. The best players travel light: empty the mind of fear and judgment, and step into each point clean.

Parent Insight:

Real growth comes from space, not pressure. Confidence is nurtured by giving children room to fail, feel, and try again—not by constantly pushing.

Sisters Kana and Kanoon at the Thailand Academy

Real-Life Transformation: Kana and Kanoon

Kana and Kanoon are two sisters from Bangkok. Their father worked at my academy, and they began training with me when they were just seven and eight years old. Though they were new to competitive tennis, their spirit and dedication stood out.

When I opened a new academy at an international school in Northern Thailand, both girls were awarded full tennis and academic scholarships. But the move was tough. They didn't speak English, had to adapt to a rigorous schedule, and had to leave behind their family and friends. Their father joined me on staff, but it was still a major sacrifice for the whole family.

Their transformation was about adapting to discomfort and embracing their struggle—not only on the court, but in the classroom, their living arrangements, and adapting to a new culture. In training, they had to let go of the belief that their physical limits were fixed. During intense drills or fitness work, they often broke down in tears, convinced they couldn't endure another step. But through those moments, they grew in awareness, which became the primary tool of their transformation.

They also had to free themselves from the expectation to win, even as they felt the weight of their full tennis scholarships. Over time, they learned to focus on the process rather than obsess over outcomes. Another crucial shift was in discipline: at first they depended on external structure, but slowly they became their own coaches—disciplining themselves with maturity and purpose.

Kana and Kanoon trained 4.5 hours a day, 6 days a week, all while balancing full-time school and weekend tournament travel. There were tears, homesickness, and plenty of growing pains, but they never gave up. Slowly and surely, I watched them transform.

When Kana and Kanoon graduated, they were no longer the shy, uncertain girls they once were. They had grown into confident, focused student-athletes who each earned overseas scholarships to study and play tennis. One became a college tennis coach, the other works in IT in Bangkok. Their story is a living version of the caterpillar becoming the butterfly—a vivid symbol of the transformation that's possible when we release limiting beliefs, embrace discomfort, and give ourselves the space to grow.

Clearing Space for Growth

Like the caterpillar must transform before it breaks the chrysalis, our mindset must also transform so that we can break free on the court. That means letting go of the stories in our minds that say, 'I'm not good enough,' or 'I will never beat that player.'

These thoughts clutter the mind. I call it "mind-fullness"—being so full of negative thoughts, judgments, and pressure that there's no room to grow. To change, we have to shift to "mind-emptiness." That's when we quiet the chatter, let go of expectations, and open ourselves to the moment. When we do that, we create space for something new to emerge—just like the butterfly.

Shifting the Narrative

As mentioned, the negative stories we carry affect our performance. A player who believes they're destined to lose may play tight and cautious, stuck in fear. They become a caterpillar refusing to leave the cocoon.

But when we release ourselves from those stories—when we shift our mindset—we can play freely. We're no longer chained to the past or controlled by fear. We start creating new experiences, new results, and a new version of ourselves. We become the butterfly.

Breaking the Cocoon

I saw this firsthand with a top-20 ITF junior, Suchanan, who later broke into the top 200 on the WTA Tour. Before a big final, she had lost three times to the same opponent. In the days before the match, we worked hard to shift her mental story—replacing "I'm not good enough" with something stronger. She walked onto the court with clarity and courage, and she won. That match wasn't just about beating an opponent. It was about defeating the limiting beliefs that had held her back. It marked a major leap in both her performance and personal growth.

Coach's Corner:

Help players identify and reframe their limiting beliefs. Guide them gently away from 'I can't' and toward 'Let's see what I can do.' Transformation often begins in the mind.

Player's Note:

Ask yourself: 'What belief do I carry that holds me back?' 'What would happen if I let it go, just for one match?' Try playing without that story—you might surprise yourself.

Parent's Insight:

Encourage effort and growth, not just results. Your child's biggest breakthroughs often come after internal struggles you can't always see. Support the process, not just the outcome

Embracing the Beginner's Mind

Another key part of emptiness is letting go of fixed expectations. This applies to both practice and competition.

Think of a beginner—someone just learning the game. They don't worry about rankings or reputations. They're not weighed down by "shoulds" or pressure to perform. They explore. They play. They're *present*.

As we progress, we often lose that presence. Expectations creep in: "I should be better by now." "I can't lose to this opponent." But these thoughts make us tight. When we return to a beginner's mindset—empty of rigid expectations—we unlock freedom and play with more ease and joy.

Naomi Osaka showed this early in her career. She played with curiosity and freshness, unburdened by pressure. That openness helped her grow fast and reach the top,

But once she reached the higher ranks, she started feeling pressure from herself and expectations. She suffered performance anxiety and stopped playing for a while. Now that she's back on court, she is more at ease—smiling and enjoying the game more.

When we empty ourselves of stories, pressures, and rigid expectations, we create space for confidence, growth, and love of the game. This is the power of emptiness. It's not about losing something but opening up to something powerful. It is the first step on the Inner Way.

The Coachable and Connected Learner

At the heart of an empowering attitude in tennis is the willingness to be coachable and open to learning. This is where the idea of *emptiness* truly manifests. You let go of what you think you already know, and step into each experience with humility and curiosity.

Michael's Journey: From Beginner to Competitor

When I was directing at a well-known academy in Bangkok, I met a young boy named Michael. He was brand new to tennis, but what set him apart was not his talent—but his attitude. He listened. He tried. He didn't let frustration or self-judgment get in the way. He just kept learning.

At first, he had the usual beginner struggles—awkward grip, inconsistent contact, poor footwork. But because he stayed open to feedback and trusted the coaching process, his improvement was rapid. Whether it was adjusting his swing or releasing the idea that he "should already be good," Michael stayed engaged. Within months he was competing with seasoned juniors.

His story mirrors the *Caterpillar to Butterfly* transformation. It's not just about improving strokes—it's about releasing the beliefs that block growth and stepping into your potential with openness and trust.

Why a Coachable Attitude Changes Everything

- **Faster Progress:** Players who are open to feedback improve faster. They're not stuck in self-defense or ego; they're focused on learning.
- **Stronger Relationships:** When a player and coach build mutual trust, the learning environment becomes rich and nurturing.
- **Resilience:** Coachable players bounce back more easily. They don't collapse under criticism—they grow from it.

How to Be Coachable and Connected

1. **Trust + Connection** Build a relationship with your coach that's grounded in honesty and communication. When you trust your coach, you're more likely to accept feedback and act on it.
- *Try This:* Do regular check-ins. Ask your coach what you're doing well and where you can grow. Share what you're noticing, too.
2. **Engagement + Self-Discipline** Be fully present when you train. Tennis improvement is a slow, steady process. Show up for it.
- *Try This:* Start practices with a short breathing or visualization exercise to clear your mind. Stick to a consistent training routine, even when it's tough.
3. **Humility + "Emptying the Cup"** Let go of the "I already know this" mindset which kills growth. Stay curious.
- *Try This:* After each match or session, ask: "What did I learn?" Focus more on what you gained than what went wrong.

Coach's Corner:

Encourage players to see feedback not as criticism but as a tool. Build trust through honesty and consistency.

Player's Note:

The best players are not always the most talented—they're the most coachable. Be willing to empty your cup.

Parent's Insight:

Support your child by praising their effort and openness to learning, not just their results. Growth starts with attitude.

Embracing the mindset of a coachable learner is about more than tennis. It's about becoming someone who's ready to grow. Like Michael, players who embody emptiness—through curiosity, trust, and humility—often make the most meaningful progress.

II. Oneness with the Game

"The only way to make sense out of change is to plunge into it, move with it, and join the dance."

—Alan Watts

The Opponent as Partner

Most people think of competition as a battle—one player trying to beat another. But the word "competition" actually comes from the Latin *competere*, meaning "to come together." This perception change can literally be a game changer.

In tennis, you're not just playing *against* someone—you're playing *with* them. Think about the legendary rivalry between Roger Federer and Rafael Nadal. Yes, they battled hard. But underneath it all was deep respect. After their epic 2008 Wimbledon final, Federer said, "I have always had a lot of respect for Rafa. He's a great champion. He's a competitor. And he plays the sport with passion." They pushed each other to new levels. And that's the point—great competition makes you better.

You can't play real tennis alone. Hitting against a wall is helpful—but it's not the same. A match becomes a living experience when you interact with another player. It's a dance: you move, they respond; they attack, you defend. That rhythm is the beauty of the game.

This idea shows up in Taoism and Zen too. In Taoism, there's a concept called *Wu Wei*, or effortless action—flowing with what's happening, not forcing things. When you flow with your opponent instead of fighting against them, the game becomes easier, more beautiful, and even more competitive.

There's a Zen story of two sword masters who meet in a duel. Instead of trying to destroy each other, they focus on the movement, the skill, the moment. Their duel becomes a dance, just like a great match. That's true oneness.

Oneness in Change: Mastering the Flow

Tennis is all about change. No two points are ever the same. Conditions shift. Your opponent changes tactics. The wind picks up. You miss a shot you usually make.

Trying to control everything in tennis is like trying to hold back the tide. It's exhausting. And it does not work. The best players don't resist change—they move with it.

Take Novak Djokovic. He's known for his flexibility—not just physically, but mentally. If a match gets tricky, he adapts. He doesn't panic or force his way through the match. He adjusts. He flows. That's *Wu Wei* (non effort) in action. It's oneness with the moment. Bruce Lee put it perfectly: "Be water."

Andre Agassi understood this too. He once said, "The only way to get better is to embrace the pain, to go to the edge of what we think we can do." That edge—the place where things are uncertain and uncomfortable—is where real growth happens. When you stop trying to make things predictable and instead say, 'Okay, let's see what happens next,' your whole mindset shifts. You stop resisting. You start flowing.

The Tao teaches us that harmony comes from aligning with what is, not forcing what is not. In tennis, that means accepting the bounce, the opponent, the nerves, the weather. All of it.

A Zen story tells of a master painter who started a canvas that was not working. Instead of fighting the paint, he let the brush go where it wanted. What came out was better than anything he had planned. Tennis is like that too.

When you accept change, you stop suffering from it. Instead of being thrown off by surprises, you start responding skillfully. And you start enjoying the match more—even when it's tough.

When you find oneness with your opponent and with change, tennis becomes more than a game—it becomes a mirror. It shows you where you're rigid, where you're fluid, and where you can grow. Again, that's what the Inner Way is all about.

Coach's Corner:

Teach players to accept what happens in a match. Adaptability is more important than having a perfect plan.

Player's Note:

Don't fight the flow—move with it. Each shot is a new chance to respond and create.

Parent's Insight:

Support your child's growth by helping them embrace the unexpected, rather than fearing it. This mindset leads to long-term development.

Oneness in Struggle: Embracing the Process

Struggle is a natural part of tennis—woven into practice, competition, and any type of growth. From learning the basics to playing at elite levels, players constantly face challenges that test their skills and mental strength. Instead of avoiding struggle, we can learn to enjoy the struggle because it is a chance to grow stronger, learn more, and deepen our love for the game.

A favorite saying of mine goes, "Rough weather makes for good timber." It reminds us that adversity builds character. The same is true in tennis: the more we lean into our struggles, the more we become resilient and refined players.

Struggle in Practice: A Path to Growth

Every missed serve or mis-hit backhand is not a failure—it's a lesson. Take Simona Halep, for instance. Before winning her first Grand Slam at the 2018 French Open, she faced many tough losses. Her coach, Darren Cahill, noted that each defeat helped her grow. Struggle, in this sense, becomes training for the heart and mind.

Struggle in Competition: Building Inner Strength

Struggle becomes even more intense in competition. Pressure, nerves, and fatigue challenge every athlete. Consider the 2019 Wimbledon final between Novak Djokovic and Roger Federer. It went to five sets and ended in a dramatic tiebreak. Djokovic has said of such moments, "It's normal to experience doubts and fears, to be negative, to be stressed, to be pessimistic in your head. But it's important to bounce back to the present moment." His ability to stay centered in struggle is what helped him win.

"The Obstacle as Path"

There's a Zen proverb that says, "The obstacle is the path." Struggle is the way forward—not something to avoid. Like Zen archers who embrace each missed shot as part of their training, tennis players can use challenges to improve their awareness and resilience.

In *One Arrow, One Life*, Kenneth Kushner shares a moment when his archery teacher told him that his pain was not getting worse, but his tolerance was diminishing. It's a powerful lesson: building mental toughness is not about eliminating pain, but expanding your capacity to handle it.

Randall & Leo at a tournament with Alisa & Vichien (Leo's father)

A Story of Grit: Leo's Journey

Leo was a player I coached from his junior years in Thailand through his college and professional career. He was never the biggest or most naturally gifted, but he had something more important—grit. He faced every challenge head-on. Even when he was tired, injured, or discouraged, he never backed down.

Leo went on to win both the NCAA Division III singles and doubles titles. He now competes on the ATP Tour, often facing long travel, low-ranked tournaments, and tough losses. Still, he never complains. He accepts the grind.

One moment from Leo's journey stands out. During a Challenger match, Leo, ranked around 900 in the world and faced a player ranked 250. He was winning until he pulled a muscle in his leg. Most players would have quit—but not Leo. He stayed in the match, lost narrowly, but grew tougher through the experience. His decision to keep fighting made it a victory of spirit.

When players learn to see struggle as a teacher, they become more than competitors. They become learners, warriors, and artists—crafting their game stroke by stroke. In this way, tennis becomes more than a sport. It becomes a journey of mastery, guided by every challenge and lifted by every step forward.

Coach's Corner:

Encourage your players to lean into struggle. Praise effort, not just results. Share stories of pro players who overcame adversity. Normalize struggle as a vital part of training and growth.

Player's Note:

Next time you miss a shot or lose a match, don't beat yourself up. Ask: "What did I learn?" Struggle isn't failure—it's feedback. Embrace it, and you'll grow stronger.

Parent's Insight:

When your child struggles in tennis, support them with patience. Encourage perseverance and curiosity. Let them know struggle is not only okay—it's necessary for real growth.

The Effective Competitor: Embodying Oneness
Prime Example: Nadal's Story

To compete at the highest level, a player must learn to be at one with the game—mentally, emotionally, and physically. Few illustrate this better than Rafael Nadal. Whether he's behind in the score or in the middle of a long rally, Nadal is known for staying locked into the moment. He doesn't dwell on mistakes or get lost in future worries. He focuses on what's coming up *now*.

Much of this mindset came from the guidance of his uncle and longtime coach, Toni Nadal. In one story, Rafa recalls losing a match after skipping practice to go fishing. On the ride home, he cried in the car. His uncle simply said, "It's okay to fish, but if you want to win, you have to do what needs to be done first."

That lesson stuck. Nadal learned to commit himself to the moment and to practice. "Some days I can be by the sea," he later said, "but today and tomorrow ... I have to practice." Nadal's mental discipline and emotional steadiness are in line with his purpose and key to his success. It's a mindset young players can learn from—how the right story and perspective can shape a lifetime of inner strength.

Benefits of a Strong Competitor Mindset

1. Persistent Patience: Oneness with Change

Growth takes time. Players who accept that will be more resilient. Rather than chasing quick results, they trust the process and focus on getting a little better every day.

2. Emotional Equanimity: Oneness with Opponent

Seeing the opponent as a partner in growth—not just a rival—helps players stay grounded. Respect for the game and for others fosters a more focused, centered competitor.

3. Calm Confidence: Oneness with Struggle

When players accept that challenge is part of the journey, they stop fearing it. They learn to respond with poise and trust in their training.

Strategies to Build Competitive Oneness

1. Mindful Presence – Emotional Regulation

Practice: Teach players to use breathing and visualization before matches. Help them stay tuned into the point, the rally, the game—not the score or the crowd.

2. Reflective Practice – Preparation Routines

Practice: After matches, reflect: What went well? What felt off? Establish warm-up and cool-down rituals that include both physical and mental prep.

3. Intention Setting – Long-Term Growth

Practice: Set intentions beyond winning—like staying positive under pressure or being a good teammate. Review those intentions after the match to build awareness.By cultivating oneness—in mindset, emotional balance, and towards the opponent—players become not just better athletes, but fuller human beings. They learn to play for something deeper than the scoreboard. In the Inner Way, this is what it means to be an effective competitor.

III. Play: An End in Itself

"You do not play a sonata in order to reach the final chord"

– Alan Watts

Playfulness is the secret sauce of true mastery. In Zen, Taoist, and Buddhist traditions, play isn't seen as something silly or unimportant— it's seen as a sign of presence, spontaneity, and being in harmony with the moment. When we play with a sense of joy and lightness, we become more relaxed, focused, and free to perform at our best— without forcing or overthinking.

In the Taoist classic *Zhuangzi*, there's a story about a butcher who was so skillful that he could carve an ox with graceful ease. He said his success was not about strength or effort—it was about following the natural rhythms of the animal. Similarly, in *Zen in the Art of Archery*, mastery comes not by trying harder, but by letting go and allowing the shot to release itself. That's the spirit of playfulness: being fully immersed in what you're doing, letting the game flow through you.

Roger Federer is a great example of this. His movement, ease, and composure under pressure reflect a deep playfulness. He once said, "I love this game. If I did not enjoy it, I would not still be playing." His joy, not just his talent, is what made him legendary.

Purposeful Play

Playfulness and commitment might sound like opposites, but they go hand in hand. Being at play doesn't equal carelessness—it means being engaged and open, without tension. As Zen teacher Shunryu Suzuki said, "In the beginner's mind there are many possibilities, but in the expert's mind, there are few."

Mansour Bahrami, a former ATP pro known for his trick shots and crowd-pleasing style, showed the power of mixing play and professionalism. I watched him play in a Davis Cup tie against Thailand, where his creativity and flair lit up the court. He made the match fun not just for himself, but for everyone watching.

Bahrami reminds us that being committed does not mean we have to be rigid. Like Bruce Lee said, "Be like water." Flow with what's happening. Adapt. Be creative. Bahrami's playfulness made him unpredictable, effective—and unforgettable.

Playfulness with Growth – Embracing the Journey

Zen and Taoist teachings remind us that the journey *is* the goal. When we fixate on winning, we lose the joy of playing. Alan Watts put it perfectly: "The meaning of life is just to be alive... and yet, everybody rushes around in a great panic as if it were necessary to achieve something beyond themselves."

Many players fall into the trap of thinking their happiness lies in winning. But a playful mindset turns every challenge into an adventure. Mistakes become learning moments. Matches become experiments. Growth becomes fun.

The Japanese word *shoshin*, or "beginner's mind," captures this beautifully. When players approach training with openness and curiosity—like a beginner—they unlock hidden potential. Rafael Nadal, despite being a tennis legend, still talks about learning every time he steps on court. That mindset keeps the game fresh and fun, no matter how many titles he's won.

Playfulness is not the opposite of discipline—it's the path to mastery. It helps players stay loose, focused, and inspired. And it reminds us all that the point of the game... is to play.

Playfulness with Practice – Finding Joy in Repetition

Zen practice often involves simple, repeated activities—sweeping, meditating, chanting—not because the actions are special, but because through repetition, we can learn presence and focus. In martial arts, endlessly drilling the same move, like a karate punch or a judo throw, builds true skill. But only if it's done with awareness—not mindless repetition.

The same is true in tennis. Too often, players see practice as something they just have to get through to get better. But that mindset drains the fun—and with it, the learning. A playful mindset turns repetition into an exploration. Instead of thinking "Ugh, another 50 serves," a player with curiosity asks, "What can I notice today?"

As Kei Nishikori said: *"The most important thing is to enjoy the process of getting better."*

When you're playful in practice, effort does not feel like a burden— it becomes a game. One that challenges you, teaches you, and keeps you coming back. Playfulness is not about being silly or avoiding work—

it's about being fully engaged without tension. It's the difference between grinding and flowing.

Coach's Corner:

Help players see drills as games. Mix up routines. Challenge them to notice subtle things like spin or rhythm. Remind them that joy fuels progress.

Player's Note:

Approach practice like a puzzle: What can I figure out today? How can I make it fun? When you're curious, improvement happens naturally.

Parent's Insight:

Celebrate effort and enthusiasm more than results. Ask your child after practice, "What was fun?" or "What did you discover?" It builds a lifelong love for learning.

Randall at Bangkok Academy with Top 10 ATP player Paradorn during junior clinic

Embodying Playfulness for Peak Performance

Playfulness is not just for beginners. It's a powerful tool for elite performance. When players are relaxed, curious, and joyful, they unlock creativity and resilience under pressure.

Take Paradorn Srichaphan, a top-10 ATP player from Thailand. I knew Paradorn as a junior—he often played against our Bangkok academy's players. Even then, his joy was unmistakable. He embodied *sanook*, the Thai spirit of fun. He smiled, stretched, and even danced between points. His playfulness did not distract—it freed him. It helped him stay fluid and focused in battle.

Gaël Monfils is another example. Famous for his electric energy and jaw-dropping shot-making, Monfils plays with freedom. His joy is infectious. In tough moments, he experiments, entertains, and flows. This lighthearted approach is not just a show—it helps him manage pressure and find the Zone.

Both Paradorn and Monfils prove that when you love the game and let that love shine through, performance rises to another level. Playfulness keeps the inner fire alive.

Coach's Corner:

Encourage expressive play. Let players try creative shots or mini-games in practice. Joy builds confidence and resilience.

Player's Note:

Don't be afraid to smile, laugh, or experiment on court—even during matches. Fun fuels flow.

Parent's Insight:

Your child's joy in the game is more important than any trophy. Support their playfulness—it keeps the sport meaningful and sustainable.

The Benefits of Developing a Playful Competitor Mindset

Playfulness in tennis is not just about having fun—it's a game-changing mindset that supports mental strength, creativity, and joy. When players adopt a playful approach to their training and matches, they feel more connected to the game, stay more positive during pressure moments, and play more freely.

What a playful mindset can bring:

1. **Joyful Engagement** – Players who focus on their love for the game (instead of worrying about rankings or results) stay more immersed and enjoy themselves more, leading to better performances.
2. **Creative Freedom** – Playfulness unlocks experimentation. Players are more likely to try new strategies and shots, helping them stay flexible and adapt quickly.
3. **Resilient Positivity** – When players stop fearing failure, they bounce back from mistakes faster and keep a lighter, more optimistic mindset—even in tough matches.

Practical Strategies to Cultivate Playfulness

If players want to bring more playfulness into their training and competition (without losing focus), try these strategies:

4. Spontaneous Drills – Create drills that invite creativity, like having a "drop shot only" point or rewarding surprise shots.
- *Practice:* Give points for creativity during match play or drills— like best change of pace or most creative angle.

5. Pressure-Free Competition – Set up matches where the score does not matter. Focus on risk-taking and learning.
- *Practice:* Play mini-sets where the goal is to try new things—slice everything, play only cross-court, or serve and volley every point.

6. Gamify Training – Turn repetitive tasks into fun challenges.
- *Practice:* Use targets on the court for serves and make it a contest. The more playful the structure, the more present the player becomes.

7. Bring Humor into Training – Lighten the mood. Celebrate creative points and laugh at the goofy ones.
- *Practice:* Do a silly dance or impersonate a famous player after a big rally. It keeps things loose and joyful.

8. Accept the Unpredictable – Embrace the chaos of the game.
- *Practice:* Challenge players to switch tactics mid-set. This teaches adaptability and reminds them that tennis is always changing—and that's part of the fun.

Playfulness is a powerful pathway to peak performance. It invites joy, expression, and freedom on the court. Just like Paradorn Srichaphan and Gaël Monfils, who bring passion and fun to their games, any player can elevate their tennis by embracing play. With creativity, curiosity, and a light heart, the game becomes more than a competition—it becomes a dance of discovery.

Summary: Attitude Foundation

In this section, we explored how our attitudes—many shaped by cultural conditioning—form the inner foundation of a tennis player's experience. These attitudes often go unnoticed but play a powerful role in either limiting or liberating a player's potential. Creating an empowering attitude helps players let go of distracting thoughts and stay anchored in the moment.

We introduced three core components that build this foundation: **Emptiness**, **Oneness**, and **Playfulness**.

These concepts allow players to move beyond limiting beliefs, stay fully present, and unlock their inner game. Together, they point toward a deeper way of playing—one that isn't just about results, but about expressing one's full self through the game.

Emptiness and Mental Reset

Emptiness doesn't mean being blank or emotionless. It means having a mind free of clutter—open, responsive, and grounded in the present moment.

When players hold on to worries about mistakes, pressure from coaches, or fear of failure, their minds become "too full." In this state, they overthink, hesitate, or try too hard. But when players learn to empty their minds of these distractions, they begin to respond more intuitively and naturally. The game starts to feel less like a struggle and more like a flow.

A quiet, centered mind sees clearly and acts without hesitation. This mental emptiness, cultivated over time, becomes a foundation for confident and instinctive play.

Oneness: Unified Play

Oneness is the opposite of separation. When players are caught in self-conscious thoughts—"Am I playing well?" "What will Coach think?" "I can't miss this shot!"—they become divided from the game itself.

Oneness means being fully engaged with the ball, the moment, and even the opponent. It's the feeling of being in rhythm, when shots come naturally and awareness is sharp. In this state, players stop over-controlling and start flowing. The mind and body move together as one, and the game plays through them.

Oneness helps players stay grounded under pressure and adapt in real time. Rather than fighting the match, they dance with it.

Playfulness: Performing with Joy and Freedom

Playfulness might sound like the opposite of being serious, but in truth, it's the key to playing your best. A playful mindset keeps tennis enjoyable, creative, and free from the pressure of perfection.

When players are too serious, they often tighten up, fear failure, or lose their spark. But when they allow themselves to enjoy the game, even in tough moments, they open the door to peak performance.

Playfulness doesn't mean being careless—it means being fully engaged while staying light and curious. Great players like Federer, Monfils, and Paradorn all showed how joy can fuel greatness.

Together, They Create the Zone

When Emptiness, Oneness, and Playfulness work together, a player can enter the Zone—that transcendent state where action flows effortlessly and awareness is sharp. In the Zone, athletes are no longer trying to win or avoid losing. They are simply present, engaged, and alive in the game.

The Zone is not a mystery. It's the natural result of a mind that's clear (Emptiness), connected (Oneness), and joyful (Playfulness). When these qualities come together, tennis becomes more than a sport—it becomes an expression of the player's deepest self.

Next, we move into the second foundation of the Inner Way: **Awareness**. It builds upon everything we have discussed by helping players stay awake to what's happening inside and around them, deepening both performance and self-understanding.

Coach's Corner:

Help players focus more on presence than perfection. Encourage them to let go of outcomes, embrace the process, and explore their inner game. Share stories, metaphors, and examples that reinforce lightness, connection, and joy.

Player's Note:

Your attitude shapes your game more than your strokes do. Practice showing up with an open mind, connecting fully with the moment, and playing with a sense of joy—even when the match is tough. That's how you grow and play your best.

Parent Insight:

Support your child's journey by valuing effort, presence, and curiosity over just wins and losses. When tennis stays fun and meaningful, your child will stay engaged and grow on and off the court.

Awareness: The Compass of Empowerment

If attitude is the engine that drives a player's performance, awareness is the compass that keeps them on course. Attitude helps shape mindset, but awareness helps players *see* what's happening in their mind, body, and environment—without judgment.

Once in a quiet temple courtyard, I watched a young monk play table tennis. His movements were light and fluid, yet deliberate. He smiled, focused. He was at play and utterly present.

This kind of playful, nonjudgmental awareness can be powerful. It allows players to notice what's going on inside and around them without getting swept away by it. Instead of reacting to every thought or emotion, they can respond with intention. That's how a player begins to shift from being a *passenger* in their tennis journey—tossed around by emotions, expectations, and ego—to becoming a *pilot* who is consciously directing their focus and energy.

Unlike analysis or overthinking (which usually creates more stress), awareness is about observing without trying to control. Tim Gallwey, author of *The Inner Game of Tennis*, emphasized that true awareness is not about judging the mind—it's about noticing it with curiosity.

Inspired by Zen, Taoism, and Buddhist teachings, awareness invites players to act without forcing, to respond without resistance. It is a way of playing that allows the game to unfold naturally. And when combined with a strong attitude, awareness helps players stay grounded in the moment and centered in themselves.

With awareness as their compass, players learn to navigate the complexities of both their outer and inner game, ensuring they stay on course toward developing and benefitting from an empowering attitude. This transformation shifts the inner journey from mere reaction to intentional, skillful action—empowering players to fully assume the role of pilot, guiding their mental and emotional states with presence, balance, and confidence. To see just how powerful awareness is, let's look at a pattern I've observed again and again in players: what I call the Perception-Projection Loop.

The Perception-Projection Loop

In tennis, how you *see* yourself often becomes how you *play*. This section explores a powerful idea called the **Perception-Projection Loop**—a mental pattern where our thoughts and beliefs shape our performance, often without us realizing it.

From a young age, players pick up messages—about success, failure, talent, and self-worth. If a player starts believing "I'm not good enough" after a tough loss, that thought can linger. Next time they play, it might show up as hesitation, tension, or fear. They're not just playing an opponent—they're battling their own beliefs.

But the reverse is also true. If a player views challenges as chances to grow, they carry confidence into the next match. Miss a serve? No problem. They recall their training, reset, and focus. That mental shift boosts their performance and enjoyment.

This loop—how we perceive, then project—is always running. And for many players, pressure from parents or coaches adds fuel: "I have to win," "I can't mess up," or "I don't want to disappoint them." These thoughts loop around and sabotage focus.

To break the loop, awareness is key. Players need to *notice* when they're caught in negative thought spirals and gently bring themselves back to the moment. Try focusing on the breath, the sound of the ball, or the feel of the racket. These small anchors can reset the mind. Mantras can also help.

Positive reinforcement replaces the old story with a more empowering one. Over time, players learn to become story-shifters—rewriting their inner script. Instead of thinking, 'I always choke under pressure,' they begin to believe, 'I get stronger every time I face a challenge.'

Visualization, breathwork, and mindfulness are important aids. They connect players to the present and quiet the inner critic. When athletes master their feedback loop, they begin to move with ease and clarity—both in tennis and in life. Of course, this kind of mental transformation is not always easy. Players might go through what feels like a tough emotional patch—doubting themselves, wrestling with fears, or questioning their identity. But this is often where real growth begins.

By reflecting honestly, players can start to see the pressures they have been carrying—expectations from coaches, fear of failing, or needing to look good. Naming these pressures helps relieve them.

As players move through this inner work, they develop resilience. They stop letting old beliefs run the show and start responding with more freedom, intention, and joy. Tennis becomes less about proving something and more about playing from a real, authentic place.

In the end, mastering the perception-projection loop means learning to step on the court with self-awareness. It's what becoming the **pilot** is all about.

Awareness. Intention. Rewriting the story. THAT IS THE INNER WAY.

Coach's Corner:

Help your players become aware of the story they're telling themselves—especially when they make mistakes. Encourage simple reset cues like deep breathing, positive mantras, or shaking it off.

Player's Note:

If you find yourself tense before a match, ask: What story am I telling myself? Choose one that empowers you. Try saying, "Every day, in every way, I'm getting better."

Parent's Insight:

Children often want to please you more than they let on. A simple comment—"I'm proud of your effort today"—can help ease performance pressure and create space for growth.

Randall (back-right) in Bhutan conducting a junior clinic for the Federation

Explorations East: A Compass of Awareness

My own path to understanding awareness started in college, where I studied philosophy at UNC Chapel Hill. That's when I began questioning many of the beliefs and mental habits I'd picked up from culture, family, and my sport.

At the same time, I was fortunate to begin my tennis teaching journey at Camp Manitou under Peter Burwash's guidance. Peter emphasized being present, being aware, and staying engaged with what's in front of you. His coaching—and his example—became a model for how awareness could be practiced on the court.

But it was not until I lived and worked in Asia for over 25 years that awareness truly became central to my life and coaching. Immersing myself in Eastern traditions—Zen, Taoism, and Buddhism—deepened what I had already sensed about the inner game. I came to understand that these traditions were not just spiritual ideas; they were mental training systems for living and performing with clarity, connection, and ease.

Zen taught me the power of being fully present. In my academies, schools, and programs across Asia, I encouraged players to quiet their minds, let go of self-judgment, and notice what was happening in their body and breath. We trained awareness through observing simple moments—feeling the grip, watching the ball, sensing the rhythm of the stroke. That simplicity helped players stay calm and focused in the moment.

From Buddhism, I shared the concept of *mind-emptiness*—not blankness, but in a way that clears space for presence. I taught players to focus on the feel of the racket, their contact point, and their breath. One of my players once came off court mid-match, anxious and distracted. I reminded them to acknowledge their racing thoughts without resisting them—and then to return to the ball. It worked. Their game flowed.

Taoism introduced me to the idea of *Wu Wei*—effortless action. In conversations with monks and awareness teachers, I learned that we don't always need to push harder. Sometimes, the best performance comes when we stop forcing and start flowing.

I remember a player trying to control every detail in a high-pressure match. I told him, "Trust your training. Let your body play." He let go—and played his best set of the tournament. That experience, and many others like it, affirmed that awareness is not just mental. It's practical. It frees players to move naturally, perform better, and enjoy the game more.

Awareness vs. Analysis

Alan Watts, one of the great interpreters of Zen for Western audiences, once wrote that awareness means experiencing the moment directly—without mental labels, judgments, or stories. When we fall under the spell of an emotion—"I'm nervous" or "I'm confident"—we shift away from experiencing it and start thinking *about* it. That's when problems begin.

In tennis, this shift is critical. Recall that player nervous about blowing a key serve. The moment they start thinking, "I can't miss," or "What if I double fault?", their body tightens, their timing slips, and instinct gives way to interference. The pressure to perform grows as the ego takes the wheel. Instead of simply being in the moment, they're caught in a quickening mental spiral.

Awareness interrupts that spiral. When players notice their nerves and *stay present*—without pushing feelings away or trying to control them—they play more freely. The fear loses power, and instinct returns.

East vs. West

In my decades of teaching tennis, I've noticed a sharp difference between how Eastern and Western traditions approach the mental game.

Western coaching often emphasizes analysis: "Break down the swing," "Evaluate the shot," "Fix what's wrong." That critical approach has value, especially in training. But in matches, too much thinking creates hesitation and tension.

Eastern philosophies like Zen, Taoism, and Buddhism take a different route: they emphasize *awareness*. Not thinking, but noticing. Not judging, but observing. This awareness leads to flow, presence, and a more instinctive, expressive game.

Awareness in Action

In my facilitating sessions, I often ask players to pause and feel. To listen to their breath. To sense the racquet in their hand. To be aware of the ball—not with scrutiny, but with openness. These are simple practices that give the player an experience, and over time, they build a kind of inner stillness that helps them perform at their best.

When a player can stay aware under pressure, they unlock a different level of performance. And that, more than anything else, is what separates good players from great ones.

As we continue exploring the Inner Way, remember this: awareness is not about figuring things out. It's about *being here*, seeing clearly, and letting the game play through you.

Peter Burwash, Randall, Paul Dale, and Mooga at Bangkok Tennis Academy

From Thailand to the Courts of Oz

Picture a young player stepping onto the court at their first Grand Slam event. The stadium buzzes with energy, the crowd is watching, and expectations feel like a weight on their shoulders. As the match begins, anxiety sets in. They start to overthink their serve, technique, footwork. "What if I mess up? What will Coach think if I lose?" Their mind races, and with each passing point, their game unravels—double faults, mistimed shots, and a loss of rhythm.

Now, imagine another player—same tournament, same court—but with a different mindset. This player has trained in mind-emptiness techniques, learning how to let go of thoughts and return to the present moment. When nerves creep in, they take a deep breath and ground themselves. "Just play," they whisper internally. They focus on the bounce of the ball, the sound of contact, the rhythm of their body. Their game flows. They stay composed, agile, and fully in the moment. This is the power of awareness in action.

I saw this difference firsthand while working at our Bangkok academy. I traveled to the Australian Open with one of our top juniors, Pramote, who was ranked 50th in the ITF world rankings. Despite the huge stage, he played with the same calm and focus he had back in Thailand. He didn't treat the moment as something overwhelming or special, he simply played. He remained composed, grounded, and engaged.

Though he lost a close match to a top-10 junior (4–6, 5–7), what stood out wasn't the result but his presence. His ability to stay calm and focused came from years of training, his parents' care, and being raised in Thai culture—which is deeply influenced by Buddhism. Pramote's Zen-like approach allowed him to play with clarity, adaptability, and grace.

Later, he went on to become the No. 1 player at Elon University, one of the best to ever represent the school. He was known not just for his skill, but for his incredible attitude, calm under pressure, and consistent awareness in competition.

Even champions like Novak Djokovic speak about this. He has said that his biggest opponent is often his own mind. In high-pressure moments, he returns to his breath and body, using awareness to stay present and reset.

When players cultivate awareness—of breath, body sensations, and non-judgmental reflection on their thoughts—they access a state of pure play. This is the "inner game" at its highest form. No longer trapped by fear or pressure, they become free to play with instinct and joy.

Ultimately, developing awareness is not a one-time fix. It's a lifelong practice. With it, tennis becomes more than just a sport. It becomes an art form, a mirror, a spiritual journey.

Five Dimensions of Awareness

To play tennis from the inside out, players must do more than just hit balls and chase wins. They must *see*, *feel*, and *sense* the game from within. After decades of coaching beginners and elite players, I have identified five crucial forms of awareness that shape a player's inner game:

1. Mind–Body: Inner Observation

This is the foundation. It is the felt experience of your thoughts, breath, emotions, and body in motion. In tight match moments, pressure may stir up nerves or self-doubt. But rather than trying to suppress or "fix" these thoughts, awareness allows you to witness them—and keep playing.

2. Reading the ball

This goes beyond "watch the ball." True ball awareness means tracking its spin, height, speed, and bounce—and sensing it intuitively. You learn to anticipate where it's going and how to respond *without* overthinking.

3. Knowing the Space

This means knowing where you are, where your opponent is, where the openings are, and how to use them. It's about understanding angles, target zones, and how different surfaces (clay, hard, grass) affect bounce and movement.

4. Seeing the Other Side

This is about reading body language, racket preparation, patterns, and tendencies. Is your opponent leaning forward or falling back? Does their grip shift on approach? Are they avoiding their backhand? Being aware of your opponent's habits sharpens your strategy.

5. Match Awareness

This involves tuning into the score, momentum shifts, and high-leverage moments. When should you play safe? When should you go bold? Situational awareness helps you play the *right* shot at the *right* time.

Training for Awareness in Five Dimensions

1. Body–Mind Awareness

- **Body Scan Exercise** – Before or during play, close your eyes and scan your body from head to toe. Notice tension, breath, or stuck energy. Gently stretch or breathe into tight areas. No judgment—just awareness.
- **Breath Synchronization** – Inhale during preparation, exhale on contact. It calms your mind and tunes your rhythm.
- **Observe Without Judgment** – Instead of labeling thoughts ("I'm nervous," "I'm off"), feel them as sensations. Watch them rise and fall without reacting.
- **Silent Play Drill** – Rally or play a game in total silence—no muttering or self-talk. Let the body do the talking. This builds instinctive flow.

2. Ball Awareness

"Watch the ball" is the most overused, under-explained advice in tennis. True ball awareness is not simply watching but active engagement. It means seeing and feeling the spin, speed, height, and direction early enough to respond smoothly and intuitively. Train your eyes to observe spin, bounce, and pace—not just the ball's location. Watch your opponent's swing for clues. This type of awareness leads to effortless timing.

Training Techniques:

- **Up-Back Drill:** Stand on opposite sides of the net with a partner and toss a soft ball back and forth. As it crosses the net, call "back" if it's high and "up" if it's low—to train early recognition, improve footwork, and reinforce instinctive movement. Once mastered, progress to racquet play while retaining the early call habit.
- **Spin & Direction Recognition:** Call out "topspin," "slice," or "flat" right after the ball leaves the opponent's racquet. Or call out the direction or depth ("cross," "deep," "short") to train real-time recognition. Focus on one attribute per drill for sharper results.

3. Court Awareness – Spatial Training

Great tennis players are great movers—and that requires a sense of space. Court awareness helps players make smarter decisions about where to hit, move, and recover.

Training Techniques:

- **Direction Calling Drill:** Before hitting, call out where you intend to place the ball (e.g., "crosscourt," "line," "middle"). This creates alignment between your mind, body, and shot. Vary sequences—e.g., down the line then two crosscourt—to simulate real patterns.
- **Play to Open Space:** During points, aim into the most open or vulnerable space. Use constraints like 'must hit behind the runner' to teach players to read the court rather than just the opponent.
- **Target Games:** Use cones or visual markers to define zones (deep corners, short angles, etc.). Create games around hitting specific targets to train intention, not just execution.

4. Opponent Awareness – Reading the Player

Winning is not just about hitting your best shots—it's also about knowing your opponent. Learn to spot their strengths, weaknesses, and emotional patterns.

Training Techniques:

- **Warm-Up Scouting:** Watch closely during warm-up. Which shots are reliable? Which are shaky, and why? Start the match with a plan.
- **Body Language Cues:** Slumped shoulders? Nervous energy? Confident stride? Read their mood and mindset—these are clues to their inner state.
- **Mirror Play Drill:** Match your opponent's style for a few games to understand their rhythm. Then break it with your own strengths. This builds tactical adaptability.
- **Shot Prediction Game:** Just before your opponent hits, try calling where the shot will go. Train your mind to read cues like stance, grip, racquet angle, and prior habits.

5. Match Situation Awareness – Feeling the Pulse

Matches have rhythms. Momentum can swing on a single point. Awareness of score, pressure, and emotional state helps players *manage* the game instead of being managed *by* it.

Training Techniques:

- **Score Awareness:** Pause at big points (e.g., deuce, break point) to reflect: Am I reacting emotionally? Am I tightening up? This teaches calmness under pressure.
- **Momentum Check-Ins:** After each changeover, assess who's got the momentum. Use this insight to change pace, re-center, or adjust strategy.
- **Situational Simulation:** Practice tiebreaks, serving at 30-40, or being down 4-5. Build comfort with uncomfortable moments.
- **Pressure Drills:** Add stakes to each point—pushups for missed shots or play in front of a small crowd. Simulate nerves and teach players to thrive under them.

By practicing these awareness types intentionally, players begin to *play the game from the inside out.* The shift is subtle but powerful. Tennis becomes less about fixing and forcing—and more about sensing, flowing, and responding.

Together, these five dimensions help players react less and create more—from surviving to thriving. By developing awareness—not just skill—players become more complete competitors and more grounded people. It's how the Inner Way turns into outer success.

Summary: Awareness Foundations

In this section, we explored the five key dimensions of awareness that act as a compass for navigating a tennis player's inner journey: Mind/Body, Ball, Court, Opponent, and Match Situation. Each type of awareness helps players stay focused, calm, and ready to respond skillfully to any moment on the court.

Mind/Body Awareness forms the base. When players understand their thoughts, breath, and emotions—without judgment—they can turn nervous energy into focused determination. This ability to stay present under pressure builds the foundation for the rest of the awareness skills.

Awareness connects directly with the first foundation of attitude. While attitude sets the tone for how a player approaches the game, awareness is what helps them see clearly what's actually happening in the moment—inside and out. An open, grounded attitude makes it easier for awareness to arise, and awareness, in turn, helps shape a wiser, more responsive attitude.

Together, attitude and awareness form the roots of the inner game.

When players combine these five types of awareness with an empowering attitude, they begin to experience the game differently—not just as a competition, but as an opportunity to grow and express themselves fully. They gain more control over how they respond to adversity and more freedom to play in the zone.

As we move into Part Two, we look at how awareness and attitude help players overcome two of the biggest internal roadblocks: desire and judgment—what I call the *fires of the mind*. These fires arise when players are too attached to specific outcomes or too harshly judge what's happening during play. They try to force results instead of flowing with what's unfolding.

Through awareness, players can learn to see the smoke before the fire arises, and adjust in real time—mentally and physically. They surrender to awareness and play with trust: in their preparation, fitness, and the rhythm of the game.

With this kind of inner foundation, players are better equipped to face challenges with clarity and courage. They move beyond the limitations of pressure, fear, and ego and step into a more powerful way of playing—from the inside out.

Coach's Corner:

Awareness training is just as important as stroke technique. Use drills that combine movement, decision-making, and self-reflection. Ask players, "What did you notice?" after key points to develop self-coaching.

Player Takeaway:

If you want to play in the zone, start by noticing more. The better you observe your breath, your body, and the ball, the easier it becomes to stay calm, confident, and connected.

Parent Insight:

Support your player's emotional development by helping them reflect, not react. Encourage them to talk about what they *noticed* in a match, not just what went wrong or right. Awareness builds emotional intelligence and resilience.

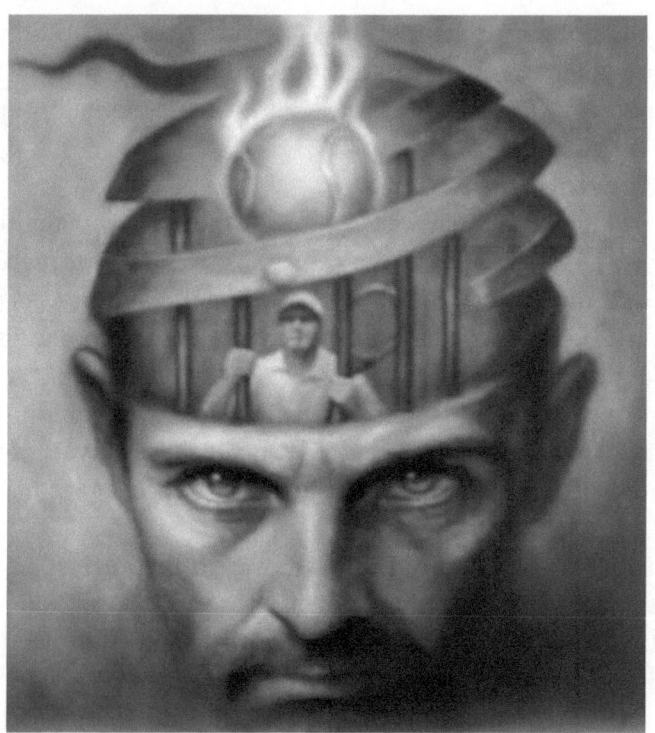

Part Two

The Inner Way:
Process and Practice

"The archer must play for nothing if he wants all his skill."

—Chuang Tzu

With a strong foundation in attitude and awareness, we now turn to the deeper obstacles that block players from reaching their full potential: desires and judgments.

These are not minor distractions. They are the core hindrances that derail performance, trigger frustration, and pull players away from the present moment—the only place peak performance actually happens.

Playing for Nothing

Desire and judgment stem from the ego. The more a player identifies with the sense of "I"—*I need to win, I can't make mistakes, I have to prove myself*—the more entangled they become in emotional reactivity. As explored earlier in the section on the **Lie of I,** this is a mental trap that intensifies pressure and clouds awareness.

The ego-self always plays for something: approval, ranking, victory. But the **Inner Way** asks the player to let go of these cravings and judgments and instead play for nothing—just like the archer in Chuang Tzu's teaching.

When a player plays for nothing, they are fully present. They're not pushing to win, not fearing a loss, not chasing validation. They are simply playing. In this state, their skills can emerge naturally—unforced and free. This is what Zen teacher Eugen Herrigel called "right presence of mind." But there are two hinderances that can flare up and jolt players out of this easeful state. Let's look more closely at these two fires:

Escaping the Hindrances: Desire & Judgement

Desire pulls players out of the moment. They begin chasing outcomes—trying to win, trying to please a coach, trying to prove something. This creates tension, anxiety, and disconnection from the game.

Judgment is the fiery voice of the inner critic. It says 'I shouldn't have missed that,' or 'I'm not playing well.' It creates mental noise and steals confidence. Instead of staying tuned in to the moment, players get lost in replaying past mistakes or fearing future ones.

Together, these two forces distract from what really matters: being fully engaged in the here and now. As soon as a player begins playing for something—approval, recognition, perfection—they stop playing from their center.

Desire and judgment can flare up from a missed shot, a technical error, or a sideline comment. They can escalate quickly if not recognized. And while desire and judgment are natural, they must be extinguished if a player wants to stay in the zone.

Next we will look deeper into how these two fires arise—and how to put them out before they burn away the joy of the game.

Desire: The Grasping Hindrance

For a tennis player, desire often shows up as an intense attachment to a specific outcome—wanting to win, achieve a personal best, or meet someone else's expectations. But when that attachment becomes too strong, its smoke can cloud the mind and disrupt performance.

The more players crave a particular result, the more they tend to worry. Their minds become restless and anxious, drifting from the here and now into "what ifs." This takes them away from playing their best tennis.

From a young age, athletes are taught to chase their dreams and push toward their goals. This isn't wrong—but it becomes a problem when their identity and happiness hinge on those goals. When desire turns into craving, and craving turns into clinging, players often lose the joy and clarity needed to play freely.

Holding goals loosely while staying deeply committed to the process is a powerful balance. Commitment means giving your all, staying engaged, and playing hard—without needing a particular result to feel fulfilled. That's how players stay grounded and resilient.

Desire burns like fire—it can fuel or consume. The difference lies in learning how to harness it.

Judgments: The Critical Hindrance

Judgment is the other major inner obstacle. It creeps in when players constantly evaluate, critique, and compare themselves— 'That shot was terrible,' 'I always mess up under pressure,' or 'They're better than me.'

This internal chatter builds tension, undermines confidence, and pulls attention away from the present. The player gets caught up in what just happened or what might happen next, instead of responding to what's happening now.

Judgments are not limited to self-criticism. Players also judge the weather, the court, the crowd, the opponent. All this labeling becomes mental clutter that keeps them from flowing.

One missed shot, one bad point, and the mind can spiral. Confidence crumbles, focus vanishes. And suddenly, the match is lost in the player's head before it's lost on the court.

Judgment pulls players out of the moment and into their heads. The antidote is *acceptance*. Notice what's happening—without needing to fix it, label it, or fight it. Just observe, adjust, and continue. Letting go of judgment does not mean lowering standards—it means freeing the mind to perform with clarity and trust.

Together, these two hindrances—desire and judgment—are the fires of the mind. They burn away confidence and flow. But with awareness and practice, players can learn to let go, stay present, and play the game from the inside out.

Coach's Corner

Help players become aware of when they're chasing outcomes or judging themselves harshly. After matches or training, ask questions like, 'What were you aware of mentally today?' or 'What might you try next?' Reframe mistakes as feedback rather than failure. Set goals, but emphasize effort, presence, and learning over results. Be mindful of your language—avoid reinforcing judgment and instead support curiosity and awareness.

Player Notes

Desire and judgment are natural, but when you hold onto them too tightly, they can become hazardous. If you find yourself wanting to win too badly or criticizing yourself, pause. Breathe. Let go of the outcome and come back to the moment—this is where your best tennis lives. You're not your last shot. What matters is how you show up for the next one.

Parent Insights

Desires and judgments often grow from pressure. Instead of focusing on outcomes, support your child's presence, growth, and effort. Celebrate their commitment, not just their achievements. After matches, ask what they learned or how they felt—not just what went right or wrong. Your encouragement to enjoy the process helps them find lasting fulfillment in the game.

Extinguishing the Fires: The Process of Recognition

"We fight the fire, while feeding the flames."

— Neal Peart, Second Nature

On the path from passenger to pilot—from feeling disempowered to becoming your own coach—players often face two invisible opponents: **desire** and **judgment**. These inner fires can cloud your mind, sap your energy, and block your best tennis from coming through.

Many players unknowingly fall into this trap. They want to perform better, so they try harder. But in trying harder—chasing a win or mentally punishing themselves for a mistake—they make things worse. They feed the flames while trying to put out the fire.

The Inner Firefighter

Picture yourself standing alone at center court. Around you are a thousand invisible opponents, each one representing a different desire or judgment—'I have to win,' 'I can't miss,' 'What will my coach think?' Every racket swing becomes a reaction to these pressures.

Even when you beat one or two of them back, more rush in. The real opponent is not just across the net—it's within. The need to be perfect, to impress others, to not mess up... These are the fires that need extinguishing.

But you can't fight these fires by force. You have to recognize them, step back, and stop feeding them.

Recognize the Flames

Just like a firefighter first identifies smoke before the blaze spreads, a player must learn to recognize the signs of desire and judgment as they arise:

- That nervous energy when you're focused on winning.
- That tightness in your body after an error.
- That inner voice criticizing you for not playing well enough.

These are the sparks. If you catch them early – without reacting, without labeling them as "bad" – you can let them go before they ignite a full-on fire.

Don't Fight – Let Go

Most players try to fight these thoughts or feelings. But that only makes them stronger. Instead:

- Notice the desire or judgment.
- Acknowledge it without reacting.
- Let it pass, like a cloud in the sky.

When you don't attach to thought or emotion, you stop feeding the fire. The mind clears, and your awareness can return to the now—where the real game is happening.

"No-mind is not absence of mind—it's full engagement without ego interference."

—Inspired by Bruce Lee and Alan Watts

Coach's Corner:

Teach players to recognize internal fires without drama. Don't say 'Don't get upset'—say, 'Notice what's happening inside. Can you let it pass without needing to react?' This trains emotional resilience, not repression.

Player's Note:

You don't need to be perfect. When that voice in your head starts shouting, try this: Take a slow breath. Say, 'That's just a thought.' Then come back to your next point. No judgment. No story. Just play.

Parent Insight:

When your child is frustrated or upset, avoid rushing in to fix it. Instead, help them name what they're feeling. "Sounds like you were really wanting to win that one." Giving language to the fire often cools it down.

The Principle of No-Mind

When you stop chasing desires or trying to control outcomes, you enter a state of "no-mind." It doesn't mean you're blank or passive, it means you're present and clear. There's no voice second-guessing, no inner critic standing over you. It's just you, your breath, and the ball.

This is where performance flows. This is the zone.

The Real Firestarter

Often, it's not the mistake that causes the fire. It is the story you tell yourself about the mistake:

• 'I can't believe I did that again.'
• 'Now I have blown the match.'
• 'Everyone thinks I'm choking.'

These thoughts turn one small spark into a blaze. But when you recognize the pattern—and let it go—you reclaim your power.

Navigating the Flames: The Inner Struggles of Two Players

I want to share the stories of two exceptional junior players I coached at my academies in Thailand—Mark and Ethan. Their journeys illustrate just how deeply these internal fires can shape a player's mindset, performance, and relationship with the game.

Mark's Story: Overcoming Self-Judgment and Pressure

Mark, a bright and driven junior player from Denmark, relocated to Bangkok to train full-time, living apart from his father for the first time. He was quickly immersed in Thai culture, excelling at a prestigious school and becoming fluent in the language. On the surface, things looked ideal— he was developing quickly, physically strong, and committed.

But inside, Mark struggled. He placed enormous pressure on himself to succeed, and his father's expectations only intensified this. Mark's mind was constantly agitated by inner judgment. In practice and matches, I saw it unfold: his body would tighten, his mind would race, and he'd try harder and harder to fix things through sheer effort.

That effort, however, was misdirected. The more he pushed, the more tense and reactive he became. Instead of helping him perform better, it made him overthink, over try, and underplay.

His thoughts became fear-fueled: *'What if I lose?' 'What will my coach think?' 'How will this affect my ranking?'* Every miss, every mistake, became kindling for the fire of self-judgment. He became trapped in a loop where the desire to succeed and the fear of failure burned in tandem.

But over time, Mark began learning to recognize these flames. Instead of reacting, he started observing his thoughts and feelings. He began seeing how tightly he was holding on—how much his identity and worth were tied to the outcomes. Slowly, he let go. He returned to the present. He stopped fueling the fire.

The results were powerful: he began playing with more ease and joy. He didn't lose his passion or ambition, but he stopped grasping. And with that, he improved—not just as a player, but as a person.

Today, Mark is a successful businessman in Bangkok, married with children, and still plays tennis—now for the love of it.

Ethan's Story: Struggling with Expectations and Overprotection

Ethan was one of Singapore's top young players. He trained at my Chiang Mai academy and carried the weight of great expectations—not just his own, but his country's. Representing Singapore abroad came with a heavy load: perform well, make the country proud, meet the high bar everyone had set for him.

His parents had the best intentions but were also overprotective. They tried to shield him from difficulties, smoothing over challenges instead of letting him build the grit to face them himself. So when things got tough, Ethan often did not have the tools to handle adversity alone.

I remember one match in particular. It was the quarterfinals of an Asian Tennis Federation 14-and-under tournament in Bangkok. Ethan started strong, but soon missed a few points, made a couple unforced errors, and them the inner fire lit up.

His body language changed. His frustration grew. His focus scattered. He was not just losing points—he was losing the battle inside.

The pressure to represent his country... the fear of failing... the need to meet expectations... they all fanned into a firestorm of judgment and desire. I could see it happening in real-time. And so could his worried mother.

Ethan wasn't aware of the score and wasn't making smart adjustments.

He was simply trying not to fail. And that mindset collapsed under its own weight. By the end of the match, Ethan wasn't beaten by the player across the net. He was defeated by the fire within. Watching him emotionally unravel was heartbreaking—not just because he lost, but because he never had the chance to play free.

A New Way Forward

Both Mark and Ethan were caught in the same fire: clinging to expectations and reacting to outcomes. But both also began learning how to cool the flames—not by fixing themselves, but by recognizing what was burning them up from the inside.

They began to understand how their mental state was affecting their strokes, focus, and confidence. They started leaning on awareness instead of willpower. Over time, they each began playing in a new way—looser, more present, more expressive.

This shift is never one-and-done. It's a process. That's why I developed what I call the 4A Process—a simple structure players can use to recognize, release, and reset in real-time.

Inspired by a metaphor I encountered in Asia—"the empty boat"—the 4A Method helps players flow through challenges without clinging, correcting, or collapsing. It's where awareness meets action. I have used this method with players of all levels—from beginners, to elite juniors, to seasoned adults. Whatever the moment demands, the 4A Process gives you a structure to follow. It transforms your mental habits so you don't spiral after mistakes or shrink in tight moments.

Next we will break down the steps. But remember this: training your attitude and awareness is not optional if you want to compete at your best—it's essential. The inner game is not separate from your performance. It *is* your performance.

Coach's Corner:

When players try harder and play worse, their inner fire is burning too hot. Redirect effort from control to clarity—ask, "What are you feeling? What are you holding onto?" This awareness cools the flames and helps them shift from reacting to responding. Build the 4A Process into daily practice so becoming a "pilot" under pressure becomes natural.

Player's Note:

When you feel yourself forcing, spinning in your head, or gripping the match too tightly, pause. Take a breath. Ask: "What's fueling me—pressure or presence?" You'll always feel emotions, but awareness shows you how to respond and stay in the match when things get tough.

Parent Insight:

Letting young athletes face challenges—without rushing to protect or fix—builds resilience. Encourage them to share what they *noticed*, not just how they played. When children feel safe to struggle, reflect, and learn, they grow stronger and more confident in the heat of competition.

THE 4A PROCESS™
A SELF-COACHING RESET
FROM INSIDE OUT

Acknowledge
Notice what's happening inside.

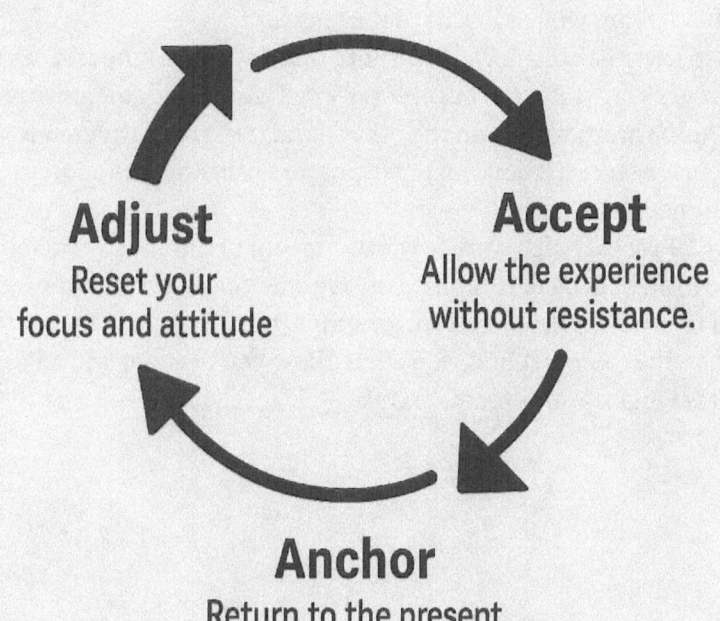

Adjust
Reset your
focus and attitude

Accept
Allow the experience
without resistance.

Anchor
Return to the present

The 4A Process™: A Self-Coaching Reset from Inside Out

At its heart, the 4A Process is about managing the two most common mental fires in tennis:

- **Desire** - craving a certain outcome or result
- **Judgment** - harsh self-evaluation after mistakes

These inner fires can burn you out if left unchecked. The 4A Process gives you a way to respond with awareness instead of reaction—helping you play from the *inside out*, in other words, where your mind and body are working in harmony.

By using the 4A Process, you're not just calming yourself down, you're learning to *coach yourself* from within.

The Four A's: Step-by-Step

If only 17 percent of a match is spent hitting the ball, then 83 percent is spent walking, thinking, reacting, and preparing for the next point. Most matches are won or lost in that 83 percent.

Neuroscientists often describe beta brain waves as the fast, alert, problem-solving state that becomes overactive and judgmental under stress. Alpha brain waves, on the other hand, reflect a calmer, relaxed yet attentive state associated with clearer thinking and more fluid performance.

The 4A Process helps you use the 83 percent of time between points to move from beta back to alpha. You cannot control the environment — call it fate, destiny, momentum, or simply the flux of what is. But you can create the internal conditions that allow you to adapt and adjust.

That is what the 4A Process trains.

1. Acknowledge – Notice What's Happening Inside

The first step is awareness. You have to recognize what you're thinking or feeling.

That might sound simple, but in a match it's easy to overlook.

Maybe you're thinking, "I have to win this game," or "I can't believe I missed that shot." You might be angry, tense, anxious—or all three.

Instead of pushing those feelings down, name them.

"I'm frustrated." "I'm caught up in wanting to win." "I'm judging myself."

This is the moment you move from Passenger to Pilot.

The Passenger is fused with the reaction. The Pilot notices the reaction.

Just acknowledging these reactions takes away their hidden power. You stop being controlled by them and begin shifting out of reactive beta mode.

2. Accept – Don't Resist the Experience

After you acknowledge what's happening, the next step is to accept it.

This doesn't mean you're okay with playing poorly or losing. It means you're not wasting energy fighting what you're feeling.

Saying, "It's okay. This is just a moment," helps stop adding fuel to the fire. Resistance feeds the fire. Acceptance helps it burn out.

You cannot change the last point. That moment is gone. Fighting it only keeps your nervous system in overdrive.

The Passenger argues with reality. The Pilot accepts reality and prepares to respond.

Acceptance begins calming the nervous system and opens the door back to alpha.

3. Anchor – Return to the Present

Now that you've softened the reaction, it's time to refocus. Anchoring is about deliberately returning to alpha — the calm, clear, attentive state where you can see the game objectively.

Slow, steady breathing helps shift the nervous system out of overactive beta and into alpha rhythm, creating the relaxed focus needed for high performance.

Between-Point Routine (20–25 Seconds)

> • Turn away from the net.
> • Take one deep breath — inhale 4 seconds, slow exhale 6–8 seconds.
> • Let your shoulders drop.
> • Walk to the line breathing in rhythm with your steps.
> • Use a simple cue: "Next point." or "Calm and clear."

Then ask one neutral question: "What's the smartest play here?"

Breathing anchors you. Alpha allows you to see clearly.

Changeover Routine (90 Seconds)

> Changeovers are extended alpha training.

> • First 30 seconds:
>   Slow breathing — inhale 4, exhale 8. Let your heart rate settle.
> • Next 30 seconds: Observe the match situation without drama
>   What's working? What needs adjusting?
> • Final 30 seconds: Choose one simple intention for the next game.

You are not reacting. You are steering.

This is the cockpit. This is Pilot mode.

4. Adjust – Reset Your Attitude and Awareness

Finally, once you are present, adjust.

Maybe you need to loosen your grip. Maybe you simplify your tactics. Maybe you shift from fear to trust. Maybe you just breathe slower.

This is action — not impulsive reaction.

From "I'm not playing well" to "I'm adapting."

From "I need to win" to "I'm giving everything I have right now."

The outcome becomes less important than how you manage yourself in the moment.

The Passenger hopes things improve. The Pilot makes small, intelligent adjustments.

Why the 4A Process Matters

Most players waste the 83 percent between points in mental chaos — replaying errors, predicting failure, protecting ego. The 4A Process transforms that time into mental training.

Each breath moves you from beta to alpha. Each routine builds emotional stability. Each reset strengthens the Pilot. You cannot control what happens out there. But you can create the internal conditions that allow you to adapt and respond skillfully.

That is the anchoring of alpha. That is self-coaching from within. And that is how you play from the inside out.

• Relieve Inner Tension Before It Controls You

By *acknowledging* and *accepting* your emotions as they arise, you keep them from building into a crisis. Frustration doesn't have to take over. Doubt does not have to spiral. You recognize it, accept it, and move through it—clearing space for calm, clarity, and competitive energy.

• Stop Craving Self-Criticism

The 4A Process is designed to interrupt the cycle of *desire* and *judgment* that so often traps players. You don't get stuck obsessing over the last point or worrying about what might happen next. Instead, you stay focused on what's happening *now*—where the game is actually being played.

- ### Return to the Moment with Calm and Power
  The *anchor* step helps you hit the reset button—on your breath, your body, and your mind. Whether it's a deep breath, bouncing the ball, or adjusting your strings, this brings you back to the present point with poise and focus.

- ### Coach Yourself—In Real-Time
  No need to wait for your coach to tell you what to do. With the 4A Process, *you become your own coach*. You know what's happening inside, and you know how to respond. That ability to self-regulate in the moment gives you a huge advantage—especially in tough matches when things start to go sideways.

Becoming Your Own Coach

The beauty of the 4A Process lies in its simplicity and immediacy. When you use it on court, you're not just calming your nerves or managing emotions. You're doing something far more powerful: you're *actively coaching yourself*.

You're no longer dependent on someone else to guide you through a setback or a slump. You're the one calling the plays—internally. You recognize what's happening. You respond with clarity. You keep moving forward.

This self-guidance is what transforms a mentally fragile player into a resilient, composed competitor. It gives you the tools to:

- Bounce back from mistakes
- Stay steady under pressure
- Shift your mindset quickly and effectively
- And play from the inside out – with presence power and purpose

Coach's Corner:

Your best players aren't always the most talented—they're the ones who've learned to manage themselves from within. They stay composed, adapt quickly, and perform under pressure. Teach players to honestly acknowledge what they're feeling; naming emotions is a powerful reset. Remind them that real adjustment is often subtle - an inner shift from forcing to trusting. That's where true growth begins.

Player's Note:

When the pressure builds and your mind starts to spin, the 4A Process helps you reset and return to the present moment. Let go of craving a win or criticizing your last shot, and you'll free yourself to just play—often that's when your best tennis shows up.

Parent's Insight:

When players learn to anchor themselves, they stop chasing perfection or fearing failure. Instead, they develop the calm confidence that allows them to play with presence— point by point, moment by moment.

From Passenger to Pilot: Becoming Your Own Coach

As tennis players, growing from passenger to pilot teaches us when to ease up and when to steer. The process begins not on the court, but within. Most players start out as passengers, heavily influenced by external expectations and disempowering beliefs. These players are often weighed down by negative attitudes and a lack of self-awareness, which hinders growth and performance.

The shift to pilot mode is about developing empowering attitudes and heightened awareness—so you're no longer just along for the ride. Taking charge of your own inner game allows you to become proactive, adjusting your mindset and applying mental tools that help you perform with purpose and confidence. Most importantly, it puts you in a better position to prevent the inner fires of desire and judgment from taking control.

This shift represents taking full ownership of your mental journey—choosing how to respond to challenges, how to recover from setbacks, and how to play with presence. It's the beginning of self-coaching.

The Fish and the Bird: Balancing Flow and Control

This balance is like watching a bird fly or a fish swim. They don't fight the wind or the water—they adjust to it. In tennis, you can't control everything: your opponent, the bounce, the weather. But like the bird or the fish, you can adjust. You can learn when to take charge and when to let go.

Players who try too hard to control everything lose flow. Players who are too passive never take charge. The most skilled athletes strike a balance: they influence what they can and surrender what they can't.

The Passenger Stage: Dependency on External Guidance

In the passenger stage, players often play below their potential. They become overly attached to the stories and identities imposed on them by coaches, parents, or ranking systems. They believe their value comes from external validation—winning matches, pleasing others, or gaining praise.

This mindset turns into a narrative they unknowingly internalize: 'I'm only good if I win.' From a young age, they're conditioned to measure success by trophies, rankings, and approval. They rely heavily on coaches or parents for direction, thinking success depends entirely on these outside forces.

But the more they chase these external markers, the more they reinforce the belief that their worth is tied to things they can't control. This leads to disconnection, anxiety, and constant pressure to prove themselves. Eventually, failure feels like rejection. Every loss stings deeper, and every mistake seems like a threat to their self-worth. Instead of enjoying the game and growing through it, they play not to fail.

From Dependency to Ownership

In tennis, we often see players who obsess over results—rankings, match scores, college scholarships—missing out on the real inner game. They neglect the skills that matter most: resilience, adaptability, and self-awareness.

Becoming your own coach starts with recognizing this cycle of dependency. Growth does not come from titles or praise. It comes from learning to trust yourself, to focus inward, and to grow through your experiences.

By shifting from outer dependency to inner ownership, players begin to navigate the game—and life—with greater confidence, clarity, and control.

The Path to Excellence: From Passenger to Pilot

Moving to pilot rank begins not just with new skills, but with a deeper shift in attitude and awareness—the two foundations introduced in Part One.

Early in their development, many players fall into the trap of seeking validation from coaches, parents, or the scoreboard. This reliance on external approval leads to inconsistency, anxiety, and frustration. Moving from passenger to pilot is about reclaiming control—letting go of pressures you can't control and turning your focus inward to what you *can* control: your reactions, your mental state, and your commitment to growth.

The first step is realizing that when you're a passenger, your mindset and performance are largely driven by others' expectations. To become the pilot, you must understand that *you* are responsible for your mindset and performance. You are no longer waiting for guidance or hoping for things to go your way—you are steering your own development.

Importantly, this shift does not mean rejecting guidance or ignoring feedback. Instead, it means learning to process those inputs through your own inner mechanisms. The best players develop the confidence to trust their instincts, adjust their strategies based on real-time awareness, and adapt fluidly to the flow of a match.

Tennis is full of variables—weather, court surface, crowd, opponent's style—but a true pilot focuses not on controlling those variables but on managing their *internal* response. This is where the **4A Process** we discussed earlier becomes essential. It equips players with a simple and powerful method to self-coach in real time. By acknowledging, accepting, anchoring, and adjusting, players learn to reset and refocus quickly, turning emotional swings into moments of composure.

Mastering this process is what allows players to transform internal struggles into growth opportunities. The 4A Process helps cultivate clarity, resilience, and a calm focus that leads to stronger performance under pressure. This is the heart of becoming your own coach—from the inside out.

This growth is beautifully embodied by players like Arthur Ashe and Naomi Osaka, who navigated personal and societal pressures by strengthening their inner resolve.

Remember: you are always both a pilot and a passenger. You influence your inner state while learning to surrender to things beyond your control. Balancing these roles is not only the secret to success—it's what makes the game deeply fulfilling. With practice, this balanced mindset becomes second nature, allowing you to play not just to win, but to grow and evolve each time you step on the court.

Becoming Your Own Coach: The Path to Awareness and Independence

Even though coaching is now allowed in some matches, the truth remains—players must learn how to coach themselves. That is what led me to shift my role from a traditional coach to what I now call a *facilitator*. Why? Because coaching and teaching often imply that you can transfer knowledge by showing or telling. But the only way to truly learn something is to experience it yourself. And experience can't be taught—it must be lived.

As a facilitator, my job is to create the right environment for that experience to happen. A drill, a game, a challenge—all repeated mindfully—*that* is the learning. Repetition is the experience.

To escape the often imaginary influence of external forces, players must reframe how they see their mistakes, their growth, and their potential. This is the shift from being a passenger—disempowered and reactive—to becoming a pilot—empowered and self-directed. This is what it means to play independently.

When players stop viewing errors as failures and start seeing them as information—just missed marks, rather than personal defeats, they take a massive step forward. Mistakes don't mean something's wrong with you. They just mean you're learning.

To become mentally independent, you must break free from the narratives that limit you. The idea that you have to be perfect. The comparison with others. The constant hunger for approval. These illusions block your natural ability to grow and thrive. As Roger Federer once said, *"You have to believe in yourself when no one else does—that makes you a winner right there."*

And here's the truth: you already have what it takes—the awareness, the strength, the clarity. It's not about *becoming* someone else. It's about *realizing* what's already inside you.

Recognizing this is how you become your own coach. Not just by managing strokes and tactics, but by managing your mind—your attitude, your reactions, your self-talk. That is the path to real growth and long-term excellence.

As Billie Jean King said, *"Champions keep playing until they get it right."* Independence is what lets players stay calm in chaos, adapt when things go sideways, and still perform at their best.

That's the goal: not just to play well, but to play *free*—guided by awareness and not restricted by pressure. That's what it means to truly become your own coach.

The Essential Role of Coaches and Parents: Supporters, Not Controllers

Parents and coaches play a critical role in a player's development—but they must recognize the line between helpful support and harmful control. At my academies, I've seen countless well-meaning parents and traditional coaches unintentionally make things harder for their players by being overbearing or overly focused on outcomes. They may want the best for the player—college scholarships, national rankings, professional potential—but in their effort to help, they often create pressure, dependency, and mental stress.

This kind of involvement may provide short-term structure but often undermines long-term growth. When players rely too much on others for motivation, direction, and validation, they don't develop the internal compass needed to compete independently. The most successful players I have worked with had support who encouraged them to lead their own journey. Their parents and coaches stepped back just enough to allow self-discovery, responsibility, and ownership to emerge.

Some parents and coaches have a hard time letting go because they want to feel needed or fear their player will fail without constant guidance. But real growth requires space. It means trusting the player to struggle, stumble, and rise on their own. It means recognizing that mental resilience and adaptability must be practiced, not handed down.

Players who are raised with a "pilot mindset"—one that values autonomy and awareness—tend to make decisions with more confidence. They perform better under pressure and learn faster because they take the initiative. They understand that tennis is a mental game as much as a physical one. As Novak Djokovic put it, "I am my own biggest competitor... I know how hard I work and what I'm capable of achieving."

The greatest gift a coach or parent can offer is presence without pressure, and love without condition. When encouragement is given without strings attached, the player feels safe to explore, grow, and push boundaries. As Richard Williams, Serena and Venus's father once said, "My job is to give them the tools to make decisions on their own."

That's what players need most: tools—not control. Independence, not dependence. Support, not micromanagement. When players are allowed to coach themselves, to face their doubts, to trust their instincts, they gain confidence and clarity. They learn not to fear mistakes but to learn from them. Andre Agassi wisely once said, "What makes you a good player is not being perfect—it is the willingness to keep learning."

Naomi Osaka's story reflects this philosophy well. Her father helped cultivate a sense of self-reliance early in her development. This inner trust helped her not only reach the top of the game but also navigate the immense pressure of being in the spotlight.

When her game slipped and she struggled with performance anxiety, those challenges became a turning point in her growth. Her ability to face and overcome that period reflects how her evolution has been as much mental and emotional as it has been physical.

Another player on the path to self-reliance is Roger Federer's 11-year-old son Leo. "I think Leo's doing great. He now also plays the occasional tournament," said Federer. "For me it's exciting to support him. I'm less concerned with results than with him having fun and making progress."

"Put trust in the coaches, the way my parents did. But you still have to keep your finger on the pulse." That's our job as parents: to support our children so they can learn to fly on their own."

Coach's Corner:

Support your players by letting them struggle and figure things out. Don't rush to fix every problem—facilitate growth. Help them build awareness, shift gears when needed, and rely less on external validation. Ask questions like, 'What can you control right now?' and guide them through tools like the 4A Process to help them become adaptable, self-aware, and confident under pressure.

Player Notes:

You're not stuck being a passenger. With awareness and effort, you can become the pilot—managing your thoughts, emotions, and actions on court. Confidence comes from taking responsibility and trusting your process. When pressure builds or you feel stuck, pause and ask: 'Am I reacting, or am I choosing to lead myself?' That shift is where real growth—and your best tennis—begins.

Parent Insights:

Your love and belief are enough. Let your child take ownership by stepping back and trusting their process. Resist the urge to fix or rescue—instead, support their growth, effort, and awareness. Encourage them to lead themselves, not play to impress. Confidence and resilience come not from constant success, but from learning to navigate the ups and downs on their own.

Part Three

Playing from Inside Out:
The Zone Experience

"The Swordmaster is unself-conscious as the beginner."

Zen in the Art of Archery

No-One, Playing for Nothing – Here and Now

The Practice of Self-forgetting

In Parts One and Two, we laid the foundation of the Inner Way-a path for players, parents, and coaches to build the subtler but essential elements of performance: attitude (the engine) and awareness (the compass).These inner skills don't just support technique, they transform the way the game is played. They shift tennis from a mechanical process into a living, expressive art.

As players develop these qualities, something natural and profound begins to emerge. The mind becomes clearer, attitude steadies. Burning desires and judgments extinguish more easily.Through the 4A Process, players learn to extinguish these fires in real-time. And then, something remarkable happens: the player no longer plays the game—the game plays through the player.

This is what we call the Zone.

In this part of the book, we turn fully toward that experience. Known as the Zone, Flow, Satori, No-Mind—this state has been described by mystics, Zen masters, and elite athletes throughout history. It's a timeless moment of total immersion, and although Zen reminds us, "He who speaks does not know, and he who knows does not speak," we still try to describe what can only be lived.

Alan Watts once said, "Muddy water is best cleared by leaving it alone." That's the essence of the Zone. It's not something you reach by force—it's what remains when you stop trying to force anything at all. It's the letting go of effort. It's what rises up when the ego recedes.

Eugen Herrigel, German philosopher and author of *Zen in the Art of Archery*, described it like this: "It shoots. It hits. But not 'I.'" Tennis players have echoed this truth. They describe shots that seem to happen on their own. Time slows, thought fades. Everything simplifies. Awareness expands. There is no fear, no doubt—just motion and presence.

Novak Djokovic has spoken of this experience: "When I'm in the Zone, I feel like I'm just a channel. Everything flows." Roger Federer has recalled matches where it felt like "someone else was playing."

This is the Inner Way in action—not controlling the game, but allowing the game to move through you. Not pushing but opening.

Not forcing but flowing.

It is no one playing for nothing in the Here and Now. This is the heart of the matter. This is the Zone.

Being the Unmoved Center

In Part One, we explored the illusion of the "I"—how much of our stress and struggle comes from trying to protect or prove the self. In the Zone, that identity softens or disappears. You're no longer "trying to win" or "afraid to lose." You're just playing.

This is not mystical. It's practical.

We were all born this way. As infants, there was no image to defend. No reputation to protect. No "me versus the world." There was simply experience unfolding. The sense of being a separate, solid "I" developed later.

Watch young children play. They are not trying to be their best. They are not obsessed with winning. They are not managing an image. They are simply immersed. Effort without tension. Intensity without fear. Focus without overthinking.

That state is not something you must manufacture. It is something you return to.

Zen, Taoism, and mindfulness are tools that help you become the unmoved center—the quiet, steady presence within you that does not flinch under pressure. You still play the role. You still compete. But you don't take the character so seriously.

When you're in the Zone, there is no one there to be afraid. No future to secure. No past to defend. You are responding, not reacting. There is no separation between you and your actions. The game moves through you.

You don't reach this state by trying harder. You reach it by relaxing into the moment and trusting your preparation. Like a skilled actor who fully embodies the character yet remains inwardly free, you play with total commitment—without being trapped by the role.

The Zone is not something you can force. But you can create the conditions for it to emerge:
• Trust your training.
• Let go of the outcome.
• Come back to the moment.
• Let the game flow through you.

That is what it means to play from the inside out.

And when you know you are not the role, there is a surprising lightness. Tennis becomes what it was always meant to be—a game playing itself through you.

Key Takeaway: In the Zone, you're not chasing success—you're allowing greatness to unfold.

When you're in the Zone, you're not playing for something in the past or future—you're not chasing a win or making up for a mistake. You're playing for nothing in the best way possible: free, focused, and fully immersed in the moment.

As Takuan wrote in *The Unfettered Mind*: "All is emptiness: your own self, the flashing sword, and the arms that wield it. Even the thought of emptiness is no longer there." This mirrors the Zone in tennis—no self-consciousness, no overthinking—just pure doing without a doer.

Herrigel, in *Zen in the Art of Archery*, echoed this: "He must learn to disregard himself... and become self-regardless, purposeless." In this Zone state, you forget about your rank, your image, or the crowd. You become fully absorbed in playing. This self-forgetting is where clarity and true freedom emerge.

Here and Now: Immersed in the Present Moment

The Zone lives in the present—here and now. In this state, you're not thinking about the score or how you played the last point. You're simply connected, engaged, and flowing.

The three fundamental qualities of this state—Oneness, Emptiness, and Playfulness—are the same qualities we explored in the Foundation of Attitude in Part One. Now, we revisit them in action.

Player's Note:

Stop chasing the perfect. When you let go of trying to win or control every shot, the game begins to flow. Trust your preparation, stay present with each ball and breath, and let the rest take care of itself. That's where the Zone begins.

Coach's Corner:

Don't push players to try harder—help them trust deeper. Design practices that cultivate presence and flow, not fixation on outcomes or technique. Encourage self-forgetting by shifting focus from results to awareness, and from pressure to process.

Parent Insights:

Support your child by easing the pressure to perform. Focus less on winning and more on being present with them. Encourage joy, presence, and growth over outcomes. Let them experience the freedom to play without the weight of expectation.

1. Oneness – Being Connected to the Game

You feel part of everything: the court, your opponent, the ball, the moment. There's no "me vs. them." It's all one dance. This connection keeps you grounded and responsive instead of reactive.

2. Emptiness – Clearing the Mind

Before flow happens, the mind must clear. No clutter. No pressure. No judgment. Just space. That space creates the calm needed for natural, smooth, instinctive movement. As Alan Watts said: "You don't grab hold of the water... instead, you relax and float." That's flow. That's tennis at its most effortless.

3. Playfulness – The Joy of Playing for Nothing

This is where effort becomes fun. You're not trying to prove anything. You're not playing for validation. You're just playing because you love it. There is a lightness to your movement, and performance flows without strain.

Benefits of Playing in the Zone

When Oneness, Emptiness, and Playfulness combine:

- You move with clarity and ease.
- Anxiety and doubt fade.
- Each shot feels effortless yet intentional.
- You stop chasing results and start flowing with the game.

The match becomes less about outcome and more about full engagement. You're not just hitting balls—you're expressing yourself. You're not just competing—you are creating.

This is the Zone. This is the Inner Way. **'It is no one, playing for nothing, in the here and now.'**

Player's Note:

Next time you practice, experiment with playing for the sake of play. Let your body move. Let go of "trying" and notice what changes.

Coach's Corner:

Design drills and games that reward presence, joy, and exploration over perfection or scorekeeping.

Parent's Insight:

Help your player find joy in effort itself—not just in wins. Celebrate their focus and growth more than the result.

Kana graduating from tennis academy & high school Alisa and Randall (far right)

Part Four

The Inner Way of Sport and Life

We often hear that "Sport is a metaphor for life," or that it teaches life skills through commitment, competition, and teamwork. While this is partly true, the deeper question is: What kind of life lessons are young athletes really learning through sport?

The answer depends on the culture they grow up in. As discussed earlier, cultural stories shape how young people view themselves, their goals, and their relationship to sport and life. These stories can either empower or limit us.

In my experience coaching in over 20 countries, I have seen how many athletes grow up in cultures where sport is treated like a battlefield. The opponent is seen as the enemy, and the goal is to dominate. But this mindset can lead to stress, burnout, and unnecessary pressure. It teaches kids that winning is everything.

But there's another way—the Inner Way. Instead of focusing on conquering others, it focuses on mastering yourself. Instead of trying to crush opponents, it's about meeting challenges with awareness, attitude, and self-trust.

As discussed, the word "competition" comes from the Latin competere, which means "to come together." In this sense, true competition is not about domination—it's about growth through challenge.

The Inner Way teaches players that the real struggle is not with the person across the net, but with our own fears, doubts, and inner noise. It's not about being perfect, it's about being present.

Whether you're playing tennis, dealing with stress at work, or facing life's challenges, the same tools apply: awareness, attitude, and the ability to reset. When we stop trying to control everything and instead focus on what's happening inside, both sport and life become more enjoyable and fulfilling.

The Inner Way invites athletes to see the game differently. It's not a battle to be won, but a process to be experienced. When you let go of the ego's need to control, you begin to flow with life—and with the game.

Winning and success are great, but when they become the only focus, they often bring stress and disappointment. True fulfillment comes not from the result, but from how you play—how present, connected, and free you feel in the moment.

This is not just about tennis. It's about life. Learning to let go, to focus on what you can control, and to trust the unfolding of your journey. That's where growth happens. That's where the joy is.

So as we close this book, I encourage you—whether you're a player, parent, coach, or simply a fellow traveler on the journey—to carry these lessons into your life. The Inner Way is about playing the game from the inside out: skillfully, joyfully, and fully present.

Let go of the pressure. Trust yourself. Play with freedom. That is the Inner Way of Tennis. And that is the Inner Way of Life.

The Pilot Path: The Inner Way of Living

Earlier, I shared how the Inner Way philosophy developed and how it shaped my experience with tennis. But the deeper impact came when I began applying it to life itself.

As a kid, I didn't realize how much my thoughts shaped my reality. I believed I was a victim of circumstance and just along for the ride. I didn't know I could influence the story I was living. That belief led to unnecessary struggles. But somewhere deep inside, I resisted the labels people put on me. I refused to let others define my worth. That spark of resistance became the seed of transformation—my shift from being a passive passenger to taking the wheel and becoming the pilot of my own life.

Then I found tennis. For the first time, I had a place where I could just show up and play—not wait to be picked or approved. Tennis became my proving ground. I practiced constantly, read everything I could, and paid for lessons out of my own pocket. I wasn't waiting for someone to hand me confidence—I was building it.

I remember a key moment: after a summer camp, I asked Coach Parham for private lessons. His response? "You're not college material." Harsh. But instead of quitting, I used that as fuel. I chose Elon College, even though it was not a tennis powerhouse, and against the odds, I made the team. That moment—seeing my name on the roster—remains one of the most fulfilling of my life. Not because someone finally said "you're good enough," but because I never gave up on myself.

Another major shift came at a camp in Ontario run by Peter Burwash. In one short session, Peter helped me improve my forehand—not by giving me instructions, but by helping me figure it out for myself. That changed everything. I realized that coaching wasn't just about fixing mechanics—it was about empowering the player to discover their own answers.

Later that week, Peter gave a talk on health and nutrition. I was stunned—at how much I did not know and how blindly I'd been trusting the world around me. That sparked another awakening. I began to question everything I'd been told. It ignited a lifelong process of unlearning and relearning.

These moments—on the court, in conversation, in silence—became the turning points that shaped my life. The Inner Way was not just a method for playing better tennis; it became a way of living with purpose and clarity. It was my journey from victim to player, from passenger to pilot.

Coach's Corner:

Don't just push players to win—teach them to master the moment. Help them stay grounded, aware, and open to learning. Empower them to discover insights for themselves; guidance builds confidence and independence far more than answers.

Player's Note:

Your real opponent is your own mind. The more you understand yourself, the stronger you compete. Choose yourself—train your mind like your forehand—and keep showing up, especially when it's hard.

Parent Insight:

Success isn't about pushing harder or protecting children from difficulty. Support their growth by encouraging inner strength, resilience, and reflection. When they learn to meet challenges, they become confident and capable on and off the court.

Evan: A Player's Experience

Throughout my career, I have received countless thank-you notes from players, parents, and coaches. But this one from Evan's parents sums up the power of the Inner Way better than anything I could write:

Hi Coach Krege,

Evan mentioned that he had a brief chat with you this evening, which reminded me that I've been meaning to reach out to thank you for everything you, Susan, and Coach Scott did for him and the team during the shortened season. The positive impact you had on Evan—both in his tennis game and in his personal growth—was truly remarkable. As you've probably noticed, Evan has always been more reserved and has never really thought of himself as a "team" player. But this year, even with the brief time you worked with him, his perspective shifted.

The way you structured the practices gave him the opportunity to connect with several of the guys on the team, and he actually found himself enjoying their company. He had an absolute blast at the party at your house and came home so excited about it—he even mentioned feeling sad that the season had been suspended. Dawn and I were shocked by how much enthusiasm he expressed, as we've never heard him talk like that after any team event in the past!

For me, that's what sports are truly about: the chance to step out of your comfort zone, grow in new ways, and build confidence.

While you and Coach Scott certainly helped Evan become a better tennis player and increased his love for the game, what we value even more is how much he's developed as a young man under your guidance. We've heard him mention the Inner Way several times as he navigates the uncertainties of the pandemic and deals with his heavy school workload.

The Inner Way has become a shorthand in our family for approaching challenges with effort, heart, and a strong mindset. We all need that right now, and I'm working on strengthening my own inner game too.

Thank you again for everything you have done for Evan. We are deeply grateful.

Warm regards, Stephen

Evan's story reveals that the Inner Way is not just a path to better tennis—it is a journey toward becoming the person you were always meant to be. This is the true essence of this book..

The Inner Way Forward

Before the caterpillar can become the butterfly, it must surrender to transformation. Before the passenger can become the pilot, he must awaken from the dream of control.

The journey of *The Inner Way* leads not by adding more, but by burning away the fires of the mind—desires, judgments, and fears—that cloud our natural state of awareness. What remains is a simpler, truer form of mastery: presence, trust, and inner freedom.

The following reminders are offered as practical tools for players, parents, and coaches walking the path from the inside out.

For the Player: Daily Mindset Rituals and Performance Anchors

From Passenger to Pilot – Compete with Focus, Play with Freedom

- **Start Your Practice-Match Like an Elite Player**: Take 3–5 deep breaths and visualize how you want to feel, practice, or compete today—calm, confident, locked in.
- **Pre-Practice or Match Reset**: Use a short routine (e.g., bounce the ball, deep breath, short phrase like "locked in") before every session or match.
- **Warm-Up with Intent**: Don't go through the motions. Use footwork drills and mini tennis to dial in rhythm and timing.
- **Between Rep Set-Point Routine**: Walk away, breathe, reset. Use this to manage nerves and stay in the here and now either in practice or a match.
- **Mistakes = Info**: Missed shots are not failures—they're feedback. Embrace the struggle and be one with is. Use the 4A Process.
- **Practice Under Pressure**: Simulate match tension. Play games where mistakes have consequences. Train your focus and be playful with what happens.
- **Compete to Grow**: Every match is a test of habits, mindset, and composure—not just skill. Be one with your competition or practice partners to pursue excellence.
- **Track Your Inner Experiences**: Be aware during practice sessions and matches of inner feelings, beliefs, and stories. Journal after matches—what worked mentally, where did your focus drop, how did you respond?
- **Be Your Own Coach**: Ask yourself in practice and matches: 'What's needed now?' Nurture non-judgmental awareness to develop your inner coach, not just your outer game skills.
- **Fuel for Life Too**: Apply what tennis teaches—discipline, composure, learning under pressure—to everything off the court.

For the Parent: Support that Builds Trust and Independence
Helping Your Player Succeed Long-Term

- **Focus on Process, Not Just Results**: Praise hustle, effort, attitude, awareness—not just winning. Practicing to practice and playing to play are empowering beliefs that need to be continuously cultivated.
- **Ask Better Questions**: 'What went well?' 'What did I learn?' 'What were you aware of.' These types of questions open growth more than 'Did I win?' or 'Why did I lose?'
- **Stay Cool Courtside**: Your calm body language = a calming signal to your child. Watch to watch so they can play to *play*. If you can't stay cool, best to observe from a distance.
- **Embrace the Long Game**: Inner and outer game skills take time. Avoid over-coaching or pushing too soon. Embrace the long and arduous process of development.
- **Let Them Struggle alot**: Growth comes from handling adversity. Don't rescue every tough moment. Reinforce being one with and embracing the pain and struggles of pursing excellence.
- **Encourage Reflection**: After practice sessions or matches, help them think through what they learned—don't give a lecture. Facilitate introspection that guides players to becoming their own coach.
- **Keep Your Role Clear**: Be the parent, not the coach. Let them own their journey from passenger to pilot.
- **Lead by Example**: Your attitude, body language, and reactions are teaching tools.

For the Coach: Developing a Pilot, Not Just a Passenger
Sharpen Skills, Build Awareness, Create Ownership

- **Expectations of Excellence**: Set clear standards for effort, performance, and professionalism from day one.
- **Coach the "Why"**: Help players understand what they're doing and why. Nurture aware, adaptable athletes who know themselves; their beliefs, desires, judgements, and stories.
- **Use Game-Based Learning**: Create drills that simulate real match demands: decision-making, pressure, movement, and the five dimensions of awareness.
- **Cultivate Composure**: Give tools for in-match resets: breathing, cue words, routines, body language, and the 4A process for extinguishing the fires of the mind.
- **Keep Feedback Clear and Simple**: Don't overload. One point of focus at a time. First ask the player questions about what they noticed.
- **Watch their mindset**: How a player responds to adversity is as crucial as their technique. Encourage mental clarity—free from excessive desires and judgments—to help them stay grounded and adaptable under pressure.
- **Model Inner Way Habits**: Show up mentally prepared, focused, and present—players follow your energy. Facilitate with an empowering attitude and be aware.
- **Listen More:** Give players a voice in their own development. Ask questions like 'What do you notice?' or 'What's your goal today?' Avoid over-instructing—too much talking is often just the coaching ego in disguise.
- **Coach Ownership**: Let them take responsibility. The goal is independence, not dependence. Help them become pilots, not passengers.
- **Build a culture of learning and awareness:** Wins and losses are just milestones on the path. Help players stay focused on the bigger picture—developing both their outer and inner game. This holistic growth not only enhances performance but also increases their chances of winning.Let this serve as a grounded, practical guide—not just for better performance, but for more complete development. The Inner Way is not soft—it's strong, focused, resilient. It turns pressure into fuel, setbacks into growth, and sport into a lifelong teacher.

About the Author

Randall Scott, a native of North Carolina, recently returned to the United States and is currently serving as the Tennis Director for the City of Burlington while also traveling on the ATP Tour with Japanese player Leo Vithoontien. With a career spanning over 35 years and encompassing 25 countries, Randall has directed programs at prestigious tennis clubs, hotels, and resorts. He has also led clinics and camps for national associations, founded and co-directed three tennis academies, and developed successful after-school programs at two renowned international schools in Thailand.

Randall worked with Peter Burwash International, the world's leading tennis management company, for five years, further expanding his expertise in managing world-class tennis programs. Throughout his extensive career, he traveled with players on the International Tennis Federation (ITF) Junior and Professional Tours, as well as the WTA and ATP Tours, working with players ranked as high as No. 20 in the junior rankings and No. 150 in the professional rankings.

A graduate of the University of North Carolina with a B.A. in Philosophy, Randall began his own tennis journey a bit later than most, yet earned a respectable junior ranking in North Carolina. He walked on to the men's tennis team at Elon College before transferring to UNC Chapel Hill, where he earned two varsity letters as a manager/ player on the men's tennis team.

After university, Randall spent 25 years living, working, and traveling throughout Asia, where he studied and practiced Zen, Buddhism, and Taoism. With over 30,000 hours of on-court experience, he developed a holistic player development philosophy rooted in simple yet highly effective "Inner Way" approaches—through experimenting on both himself and the players he has developed. In his journey he has guided over 9,000 players, from club and resort levels, to internationally ranked juniors, collegiate athletes, and senior competitors. Some players he has facilitated include elite, ITF juniors, college scholarship recipients, WTA/ATP professionals, Olympians, and Davis Cup, Fed Cup, and Asian Games players. *The Inner Way of Tennis, Sport, and Life – Playing the Game from Inside Out* is his account of this journey.

Photo Gallery

After training session with Thailand Davis Cup Team Randall (far left) and Paul Dale (far right)

Randall with Family Friend Chung in South Korea

1988-89 North Carolina Men's Tennis Team

Front Row: David Pollack, John Bristow, David Kessler, Carter Griffin, Don Johnson, Jimmy Weilbaecher, James Krege, Thomas Tanner.
Back Row: Head Coach Allen Morris, Manager Randy Scott, Andre Janasik, Chris Mumford, David Sussman, Joe Frierson, Bryan Jones, Manager Mike Fitzsimons, Assistant Coach Neil Alderman.

UNC Men's Tennis Team – Randall (top row- left)

Wilson-PBI Clinic in Phillipines for National Team Randall (back row-center)

Randall (far right) in Brunei with Thai Juniors at ITF Event

Randall in Japan with junior player Yuta

Manitou Boys at PBI Annual Meeting – Randall (center)

Randall (far left) after junior clinic in Kunming, China

Randall's Farewell Lunch with Guam Hilton Club Members

Randall and Joel Johnson at Queen's Club, England

Guam Hilton Tennis Club Junior Team- Randall (front-middle)

Kimoko Date – Top 10 WTA player with Randall after an academy clinic

www.ingramcontent.com/pod-product-compliance
Lightning Source LLC
Chambersburg PA
CBHW020742130626

46554CB00006B/2107